CONTENTS

INTRODUCTION

Since the *Edmonds Cookery Book* was first published in 1907 the Edmonds name has become synonymous with economical, great-tasting, easy-to-prepare and nutritious food. Today Edmonds continues to keep old Kiwi favourites alive while also responding with flair and imagination to the influences of international cuisines, reflecting the evolving tastes of New Zealanders in a fast-changing world.

Edmonds Everyday is big on tradition, and big on flavour. The recipes, all accompanied by mouth-watering photography, have been carefully selected from a range of previously published Edmonds cookbooks to bring some of the very best under one cover. The four baking sections are crammed with traditional recipes including grand old classics — Afghans, Louise Cake, Chocolate Chip and Anzac Biscuits — as well as many exciting contemporary cakes, biscuits and slices. The Main Meals and Barbecues chapter contains numerous dishes to suit all occasions, whether that be everyday family meals or impressive dishes for easy entertaining, many utilising international ingredients that are fast becoming staple items in New Zealand kitchens. The dishes offered in the Breakfast, Finger Food, Salads, and Light Meals and Soups sections are as flavoursome as they are varied. To give that extra helping-hand, there are also some great menu suggestions for special celebratory or festive meals.

The book is beautifully rounded off with tempting desserts — warming steamed puddings and crumbles, old-fashioned pies and tarts, as well as fresh and fruity cool desserts for the hotter months. Handy sections on Preserves, and also Icings, Pastries, Dressings and Sauces, ensure that the art of preserving and of making luscious jams and chutneys and of pastry-making is not lost to new generations of cooks.

Edmonds Everyday is another indispensable cookbook from the team at Edmonds.

CAKES

ALMOND CRUMBLE CAKE

CRUMBLE TOPPING
½ cup Edmonds standard grade flour
2 tablespoons brown sugar
70 g packet sliced almonds
¼ cup melted butter

CAKE
125 g butter, softened
¾ cup caster sugar
2 eggs
¼ teaspoon almond essence
1½ cups Edmonds standard grade flour
2 teaspoons Edmonds baking powder
70 g packet ground almonds
1 cup milk

To make the topping, combine all ingredients in a bowl. Mix well. To make the cake, cream butter and sugar until light and fluffy. Add eggs one at a time, beating well after each addition. Beat in essence. Sift together flour and baking powder. Fold into creamed mixture alternately with ground almonds and milk. Spoon into a greased 20 cm round cake tin that has the base lined with baking paper. Scatter crumble topping over cake. Bake at 180°C for 50–55 minutes or until a skewer inserted in the centre of the cake comes out clean. Leave cake in tin for 15 minutes before turning onto a wire rack to cool.

APPLE SULTANA CAKE

1 cup sultanas
2 cups peeled, cored and diced apple
  (2 medium apples)
1¼ cups water
1 teaspoon Edmonds baking soda
125 g butter, softened
1 cup sugar
1 egg
1 teaspoon vanilla essence
2 cups Edmonds standard grade flour
1 teaspoon Edmonds baking powder
1 teaspoon cinnamon

Combine sultanas, apple and water in a saucepan. Bring to the boil over a low heat. Simmer for 3–4 minutes. Remove from heat. Stir in baking soda. Allow mixture to cool. Cream butter and sugar until light and fluffy. Add egg and beat well. Beat in vanilla essence. Sift together flour, baking powder and cinnamon. Fold apple mixture and dry ingredients alternately into creamed mixture. Transfer to a greased 22 cm round cake tin that has the base lined with baking paper. Bake at 180°C for 1 hour or until a skewer inserted in centre of cake comes out clean. Leave cake in tin for 10 minutes before turning onto a wire rack to cool.

BANANA CAKE

125 g butter, softened
¾ cup sugar
2 eggs
1 cup mashed banana
1 teaspoon Edmonds baking soda
2 tablespoons hot milk
2 cups Edmonds standard grade flour
1 teaspoon Edmonds baking powder
Chocolate or Lemon Icing
   (see page 223)

Cream butter and sugar until light and fluffy. Add eggs one at a time, beating well after each addition. Add mashed banana and mix thoroughly. Stir baking soda into hot milk and add to creamed mixture. Sift flour and baking powder together. Stir into mixture. Spoon into a 20 cm round cake tin lined on the base with baking paper. Bake at 180°C for 50 minutes or until cake springs back when lightly touched. Leave in tin for 10 minutes before turning out onto a wire rack. The mixture can also be baked in two 20 cm round sandwich tins at 180°C for 25 minutes. When cold, ice with Lemon or Chocolate Icing or dust with icing sugar. The two cakes can be filled with whipped cream and sliced banana.

BOILED FRUIT CAKE

500 g mixed fruit
water
250 g butter
1½ cups sugar
3 eggs, beaten
3 cups Edmonds standard grade flour
4 teaspoons Edmonds baking powder
½ teaspoon almond essence
½ teaspoon vanilla essence

Put mixed fruit in a large saucepan. Add just enough water to cover. Cover and bring to the boil. Remove from heat. Stir in butter and sugar, stirring constantly until butter has melted. Allow to cool. Beat in eggs. Sift flour and baking powder into fruit mixture, stirring to combine. Stir in almond and vanilla essences. Line a 23 cm square cake tin with two layers of brown paper followed by one layer of baking paper. Spoon mixture into cake tin. Bake at 160°C for 1–1½ hours or until an inserted skewer comes out clean when tested. Leave in tin for 10 minutes before turning out onto a wire rack.

BUTTER CAKE

225 g butter, softened
1½ teaspoons vanilla essence
1¼ cups sugar
3 eggs
2¼ cups Edmonds standard grade flour
4½ teaspoons Edmonds baking powder
1¼ cups milk, approximately
icing sugar

Cream butter, vanilla essence and sugar until light and fluffy. Add eggs one at a time, beating well after each addition. Sift flour and baking powder together. Fold into creamed mixture. Add sufficient milk to give a soft dropping consistency. Spoon mixture into a deep 20 cm round cake tin lined on the base with baking paper. Bake at 180°C for 35–40 minutes or until cake springs back when lightly touched. Leave in tin for 10 minutes before turning out onto a wire rack. When cold, dust with icing sugar.

LEMON SYRUP CAKE

To make syrup, gently heat 3 tablespoons of lemon juice and ¼ cup sugar together, stirring until sugar has dissolved. Spoon cake mixture into a 22 cm loaf tin lined on the bottom with baking paper. After cooking cake, spoon hot syrup over hot cake. Leave in tin until cold.

CAPPUCCINO CAKE

150 g butter
¾ cup sugar
3 egg yolks
1½ cups Edmonds standard grade flour
2 teaspoons Edmonds baking powder
½ cup strong black coffee
1 teaspoon cinnamon

TOPPING
3 egg whites
¾ cup sugar

Melt butter in a saucepan large enough to mix all the ingredients. Remove from heat and stir in sugar and egg yolks. Fold in sifted flour and baking powder alternately with coffee. Place mixture in a 20 cm round cake tin lined with baking paper. Spread topping over. Bake at 180°C for 45–50 minutes or until an inserted skewer comes out clean. Cool in tin before turning out onto a wire rack. Dust with cinnamon.

TOPPING
Beat egg whites until stiff. Gradually beat in sugar and continue beating until mixture is thick.

ALMOND CRUMBLE CAKE ≫ 2

5 ≪ CAPPUCCINO CAKE

CARROT CAKE ≫ 7

7 ≪ CHERRY ALMOND CAKE

CARROT CAKE

3 eggs
1 cup sugar
¾ cup canola oil
2 cups Edmonds standard grade flour
1 teaspoon Edmonds baking powder
1 teaspoon Edmonds baking soda
½ teaspoon cinnamon
3 cups grated carrot
¾ cup (225 g can) drained
   unsweetened crushed pineapple
½ cup chopped walnuts
1 teaspoon grated orange zest
Cream Cheese Icing (see page 223)

Beat together eggs and sugar for 5 minutes until thick. Add oil and beat for 1 minute. Sift flour, baking powder, baking soda and cinnamon. Combine carrot, pineapple, walnuts and orange zest. Fold into egg mixture. Fold in dry ingredients. Grease a deep 20 cm ring tin. Line the base with baking paper. Spoon mixture into tin. Bake at 180°C for 50–55 minutes or until a skewer inserted in the centre of the cake comes out clean. Leave in tin for 10 minutes before turning out onto a wire rack. When cold, spread with Cream Cheese Icing.

CHERRY ALMOND CAKE

½ cup ground almonds
butter, melted for greasing
200 g butter, softened
1 cup sugar
3 eggs
1 teaspoon almond essence
2 cups Edmonds standard grade flour
3 teaspoons Edmonds baking powder
¾ cup milk
1 cup chopped glacé cherries

Sprinkle ground almonds over the base of a frying pan and heat gently until lightly golden. Grease a 22 cm fancy ring mould generously with melted butter. Toss almonds in tin to coat the base and sides. Cream second measure of butter and sugar until light and fluffy. Beat in eggs one at a time, beating well after each addition. Mix in almond essence. Sift flour and baking powder together. Fold into creamed mixture alternately with the milk. Mix in cherries. Spoon mixture into prepared tin. Bake at 160°C for 50–60 minutes or until cake springs back when lightly touched. Leave in tin for 10 minutes before turning out onto a wire rack.

CHOCOLATE CHIP SPECKLE CAKE

175 g butter, softened
1½ cups sugar
4 eggs
1 teaspoon vanilla essence
1½ cups Edmonds standard grade flour
1½ teaspoons Edmonds baking powder
¾ cup chocolate chips

NOTE: A 22 cm round fancy ring mould tin can be used instead of a baba tin.

Cream butter and sugar until light and fluffy. Add eggs one at a time, beating well after each addition. Beat in vanilla essence. Sift together flour and baking powder. Fold into creamed mixture with chocolate chips. Spoon mixture into a well-greased 22 cm round baba tin. Bake at 180°C for 55–60 minutes or until a skewer inserted in the centre of the cake comes out clean. Leave cake in tin for 10 minutes before turning onto a wire rack.

CINNAMON CREAM OYSTERS OR FINGERS

2 eggs
¼ cup sugar
2 teaspoons golden syrup
6 tablespoons Edmonds standard
    grade flour
½ teaspoon Edmonds baking powder
¼ teaspoon Edmonds baking soda
1 teaspoon cinnamon
½ teaspoon ground ginger
whipped cream

Beat eggs and sugar until thick. Add golden syrup and beat well. Sift flour, baking powder, baking soda, cinnamon and ginger together. Fold dry ingredients into egg mixture. Spoon small amounts of mixture into greased sponge oyster or sponge finger tins. Bake at 200°C for 10–12 minutes or until the surface springs back when lightly touched. When cold, cut oysters open with a sharp knife and fill with whipped cream.

COCONUT CAKE

250 g butter, softened
1½ cups caster sugar
4 eggs
1 teaspoon vanilla essence
2 cups Edmonds standard grade flour
2 teaspoons Edmonds baking powder
1 cup coconut
White Icing (see page 223)
toasted thread coconut to garnish
    (see page 230)

Cream butter and sugar until light and fluffy. Add eggs one at a time, beating well after each addition. Beat in vanilla essence. Sift together flour and baking powder. Fold dry ingredients and coconut into creamed mixture. Spoon into a greased deep 24 cm round ring tin that has the base lined with baking paper. Bake at 180°C for 45 minutes or until a skewer inserted in the cake comes out clean. Leave cake in tin for 10 minutes before turning onto a wire rack. When cold, spread with White Icing and garnish with toasted coconut.

COFFEE CAKE

250 g butter, softened
1½ cups caster sugar
3 eggs
2 cups Edmonds standard grade flour
2 teaspoons Edmonds baking powder
2 tablespoons coffee and chicory
    essence
¾ cup milk
Coffee Icing (see page 223)

Cream butter and sugar until light and fluffy. Add eggs one at a time, beating well after each addition. Sift together flour and baking powder. Combine essence and milk. Fold dry ingredients and milk alternately into creamed mixture. Spoon into a deep 22 cm round cake tin that has the base lined with baking paper. Bake at 180°C for 50–55 minutes or until a skewer inserted in the centre of the cake comes out clean. Leave cake in tin for 10 minutes before turning onto a wire rack. When cold, spread with Coffee Icing.

CHOCOLATE CHIP SPECKLE CAKE » 7

8 « CINNAMON CREAM OYSTERS OR FINGERS

COCONUT CAKE » 8

8 « COFFEE CAKE

CONTINENTAL APPLE CAKE

250 g butter, melted
1¼ cups sugar
3¼ cups Edmonds standard grade flour
6 teaspoons Edmonds baking powder
4 eggs
2 large Granny Smith apples, peeled
   and sliced
½ cup sultanas
2 tablespoons sugar
2 teaspoons cinnamon
1 teaspoon almond essence
icing sugar
whipped cream or yoghurt to serve

Put butter, first measure of sugar, flour, baking powder and eggs into a bowl. Beat with an electric mixer on high speed until smooth. In a separate bowl, combine apple slices, sultanas, second measure of sugar, cinnamon and almond essence. Spoon two-thirds of the batter into a 25 cm round cake tin lined with baking paper. Arrange the apple mixture on top. Spoon remaining batter over apple mixture. Bake at 180°C for 1¼ hours or until cake springs back when lightly touched. Leave in tin for 10 minutes before turning out onto a wire rack. Dust with icing sugar and serve with whipped cream or yoghurt.

DATE CAKE

125 g butter, softened
½ cup sugar
1 tablespoon lemon juice
¼ teaspoon grated lemon zest
2 eggs
1½ cups Edmonds standard grade flour
1 teaspoon Edmonds baking powder
¼ cup milk
¾ cup pitted, chopped dates
icing sugar to dust

Cream butter, sugar, lemon juice and zest until light and fluffy. In a separate bowl, beat eggs until thick. Sift flour and baking powder together. Fold dry ingredients into creamed mixture alternately with eggs. Fold in milk and dates. Transfer to a greased 18 cm round ring tin that has the base lined with baking paper. Bake at 180°C for 30–40 minutes or until cake springs back when lightly touched. Leave in tin for 10 minutes before turning onto a wire rack. Just before serving, dust with icing sugar.

GINGER ALE FRUIT CAKE

1¼ cups sultanas
1¼ cups halved pitted dates
1¼ cups currants
1¼ cups raisins
¼ cup mixed peel
300 ml ginger ale
225 g butter, softened
1 cup sugar
4 eggs
2 cups Edmonds standard grade flour
1 teaspoon Edmonds baking powder
¼ teaspoon grated lemon zest
½ teaspoon vanilla essence
½ teaspoon almond essence

Combine sultanas, dates, currants, raisins and peel with the ginger ale in a large bowl. Cover and stand in a warm place overnight. The next day, cream butter and sugar until light and fluffy. Add eggs one at a time, beating well after each addition. Sift flour and baking powder together. Stir into creamed mixture. Add soaked fruit mixture, lemon zest, vanilla and almond essences. Stir well. Line a 20 cm square or 23 cm round cake tin with two layers of brown paper followed by one layer of baking paper. Spoon mixture into tin. Bake at 140°C for 3 hours or until an inserted skewer comes out clean. Cool in tin.

GINGER CAKE

125 g butter, softened
½ cup sugar
3 tablespoons golden syrup
2 cups Edmonds standard grade flour
1 teaspoon Edmonds baking powder
1 teaspoon ground ginger
1 teaspoon mixed spice
2 eggs, beaten
¼ cup chopped crystallised ginger
¼ cup chopped walnuts
¼ cup sultanas
1 teaspoon Edmonds baking soda
1 cup milk
White Icing (see page 223)
chopped crystallised ginger to garnish

Cream butter, sugar and golden syrup until light and fluffy. Sift flour, baking powder, ground ginger and mixed spice together. Add sifted dry ingredients to creamed mixture alternately with beaten eggs. Stir in chopped ginger, walnuts and sultanas. Dissolve baking soda in the milk and stir into mixture. Line a 20 cm square cake tin with baking paper. Pour mixture into tin. Bake at 180°C for 35 minutes. Leave in tin for 10 minutes before turning onto a wire rack. When cold, spread with White Icing. Garnish with crystallised ginger.

GINGERBREAD

125 g butter, softened
½ cup brown sugar
1 cup golden syrup
1 egg
2¼ cups Edmonds standard grade flour
¼ teaspoon salt
1½ teaspoons Edmonds baking soda
1½ teaspoons ground ginger
1 teaspoon cinnamon
¾ cup milk

Cream butter and sugar in a bowl until light and fluffy. Warm golden syrup slightly until runny. Beat into creamed mixture. Add egg. Beat well. Sift flour, salt, baking soda, ginger and cinnamon together. Stir into creamed mixture alternately with milk. Pour mixture into a 23 cm square cake tin lined with baking paper. Bake at 180°C for 55–60 minutes. Leave in tin for 10 minutes before turning out onto a wire rack.

LADYSMITH CAKE

175 g butter, softened
¾ cup sugar
3 eggs
1½ cups Edmonds standard grade flour
1 teaspoon Edmonds baking powder
2 teaspoons cinnamon
¼ cup raspberry jam
¼ cup chopped nuts

Cream butter and sugar until light and fluffy. In a separate bowl beat eggs until thick. Sift flour and baking powder together. Add to creamed mixture alternately with the eggs. Transfer one third of the mixture to a bowl. Stir in cinnamon. Reserve the remaining mixture. Spoon cinnamon mixture into an 18 cm square cake tin lined with baking paper. Spread surface with raspberry jam. Top with reserved mixture. Sprinkle the top with chopped nuts. Bake at 180°C for 50 minutes or until cake springs back when lightly touched. Leave in tin for 10 minutes before turning out onto a wire rack.

LAMINGTONS

MAKES 20

200 g sponge
Chocolate Icing
coconut

CHOCOLATE ICING
2 tablespoons cocoa
6 tablespoons boiling water
25 g butter, melted
2¼ cups icing sugar
¼ teaspoon vanilla essence

Make or purchase sponge the day before required. Cut sponge into 4 cm squares. Dip each square in the chocolate icing. Roll in coconut. Leave to dry.

CHOCOLATE ICING
Dissolve cocoa in boiling water and combine with the butter. Sift icing sugar into a bowl. Add cocoa mixture. Add vanilla and stir until well combined.

LEMON CURD AND YOGHURT CAKE

250 g butter, softened
1½ cups caster sugar
4 eggs
finely grated zest of 1 lemon
2 cups Edmonds standard grade flour
2 teaspoons Edmonds baking powder
½ cup Lemon Curd (see page 223)
¾ cup natural unsweetened yoghurt
icing sugar to dust
citrus leaves to garnish
whipped cream to serve

Cream butter and sugar until light and fluffy. Add eggs one at a time, beating well after each addition. Beat in lemon zest. Sift flour and baking powder together. Combine Lemon Curd and yoghurt. Fold dry ingredients into creamed mixture alternately with lemon curd mixture. Spoon into a deep 22 cm round cake tin that has been greased and lined with baking paper. Bake at 180°C for 50–55 minutes. Cool in tin. Dust with icing sugar and garnish with citrus leaves. Serve with whipped cream.

MOIST APPLE WALNUT CAKE

4 eggs
2 cups sugar
1 cup canola oil
1 cup roughly chopped walnuts
2 cups grated unpeeled Granny Smith
   apple (2 medium apples)
440 g can unsweetened crushed
   pineapple, drained
2 cups Edmonds standard grade flour
1½ teaspoons Edmonds baking powder
¾ teaspoon Edmonds baking soda
2 teaspoons cinnamon
1 teaspoon mixed spice
Cream Cheese Icing (see page 223)
chopped walnuts to garnish

Using a wooden spoon, beat together eggs, sugar and oil until sugar dissolves. Stir in walnuts, apple and pineapple. Combine flour, baking powder, soda and spices. Stir into egg mixture. Transfer to a greased deep 20 cm square cake tin that has the base lined with baking paper. Bake at 180°C for 1¼ hours. Leave cake in tin for 15 minutes before transferring to a wire rack. When cold, spread with Cream Cheese Icing and garnish with chopped walnuts.

CONTINENTAL APPLE CAKE » 11

15 » LEMON CURD AND YOGHURT CAKE

MUD CAKE » 17

18 » ONE-EGG CHOCOLATE CAKE

MOIST CHOCOLATE CAKE

250 g butter, softened
1½ cups caster sugar
4 eggs
1 teaspoon vanilla essence
100 g dark chocolate buttons, drops or
   chips, melted
1½ cups Edmonds standard grade flour
2 teaspoons Edmonds baking powder
½ cup cocoa
1 cup (250 g) sour cream
Melted Chocolate Icing (see page 223)

Cream butter and sugar until light and fluffy. Add eggs one at a time, beating well after each addition. Beat in vanilla essence and melted chocolate. Sift together flour, baking powder and cocoa. Fold sifted ingredients and sour cream alternately into creamed mixture. Transfer to a greased 24 cm round cake tin that has the base lined with baking paper. Bake at 180°C for 70 minutes, or until cake springs back when lightly pressed. Leave cake in tin for 10 minutes before turning onto a wire rack to cool. When cold, cut cake in half. Spread bottom half with Melted Chocolate Icing. Sandwich together with remaining half of cake.

MUD CAKE

BASE
200 g packet Chocolate Thin biscuits
75 g butter
½ cup chocolate hazelnut spread

CAKE
50 g butter
1 cup sugar
3 eggs
1 tablespoon vanilla essence
1½ cups Edmonds standard grade flour
3 teaspoons Edmonds baking powder
3 tablespoons cocoa
¼ cup boiling water
¼ cup milk
icing sugar
chocolate sauce

Crush biscuits into fine crumbs. Melt butter and mix into biscuit crumbs. Press into the base of a 20 cm round cake tin lined with baking paper. Spread with hazelnut spread. Pour cake mixture over. Bake at 180°C for 45–50 minutes or until cake springs back when lightly touched. Cool in tin for 10 minutes before turning out onto a wire rack. Dust with icing sugar and serve with ready-made chocolate sauce.

CAKE
Melt butter in a saucepan large enough to mix all the ingredients. Remove from heat. Mix in sugar, eggs and vanilla essence. Mix until combined. Sift flour and baking powder together. Mix cocoa into boiling water. Fold into butter mixture with sifted ingredients and milk.

ONE-EGG CHOCOLATE CAKE

50 g butter
1 tablespoon golden syrup
1 egg
½ cup sugar
1 tablespoon cocoa
1 cup Edmonds standard grade flour
1 teaspoon Edmonds baking powder
few drops vanilla essence
1 teaspoon Edmonds baking soda
¾ cup milk
Chocolate Icing (see page 223)

Melt butter and golden syrup in a saucepan large enough to mix all ingredients. Add egg and sugar and beat well. Sift cocoa, flour and baking powder together. Fold sifted ingredients and vanilla into egg mixture. Dissolve baking soda in milk. Fold into egg mixture. Pour mixture into two 20 cm sponge sandwich tins lined with baking paper. Bake at 190°C for 30 minutes or until cake springs back when lightly touched. Leave in tin for 5 minutes before turning out onto a wire rack. When cold, ice with Chocolate Icing.

ORANGE CAKE

175 g butter, softened
¾ cup sugar
2 teaspoons grated orange zest
3 eggs
1¼ cups Edmonds standard grade flour
1 teaspoon Edmonds baking powder
Orange Icing (see page 223)

Cream butter and sugar. Add orange zest. Beat eggs until thick and add alternately with sifted flour and baking powder. Pour into a 20 cm ring tin lined with baking paper. Bake at 180°C for about 40 minutes or until cake springs back when lightly touched. Cool in tin for 10 minutes before turning out onto a wire rack. When cold, ice with Orange Icing.

ORANGE POLENTA CAKE

125 g butter, softened
1 cup caster sugar
2 eggs
finely grated zest of 1 orange
¼ cup freshly squeezed orange juice
¼ cup orange marmalade
1 cup Edmonds standard grade flour
1 teaspoon Edmonds baking powder
½ cup polenta (cornmeal)
70 g packet ground almonds
½ cup milk
orange zest to garnish

Cream butter and sugar until light and fluffy. Add eggs one at a time, beating well after each addition. Beat in orange zest, juice and marmalade. Sift flour and baking powder together. Fold flour, polenta, almonds and milk into creamed mixture. Spoon into a 20 cm round cake tin that has been greased and lined with baking paper. Bake at 180°C for 45 minutes or until a skewer inserted in the centre of the cake comes out clean. Leave cake in tin for 10 minutes before turning onto a wire rack. Garnish with julienned orange zest.

MOIST APPLE WALNUT CAKE ∥ 15

ORANGE POLENTA CAKE ∥ 18

PLUM CAKE

200 g butter, softened
1 cup caster sugar
3 eggs
1 teaspoon vanilla essence
2 cups Edmonds standard grade flour
2 teaspoons Edmonds baking powder
70 g packet ground almonds
½ cup (125 g) sour cream
½ cup milk
6–8 firm, ripe plums, stoned and
    quartered
icing sugar to dust

Cream butter and sugar until light and fluffy. Add eggs one at a time, beating well after each addition. Beat in vanilla essence. Sift together flour and baking powder. Fold flour, almonds, sour cream and milk into creamed mixture. Spoon half of this batter over the bottom of a 22 cm round cake tin that has the base lined with baking paper. Arrange plums on top of the batter. Cover with remaining mixture. Bake at 160°C for 70 minutes or until cake springs back when pressed lightly. Leave cake in tin for 10 minutes before transferring to a cake rack. Just before serving, dust cake with icing sugar.

RHUBARB AND PECAN CRUST CAKE

TOPPING
1 cup diced rhubarb
¾ cup toasted pecan nuts, roughly
    chopped
½ cup Edmonds standard grade flour
½ cup brown sugar
1 teaspoon ground ginger
75 g butter, melted

CAKE
125 g butter, softened
1 cup caster sugar
2 eggs
1 teaspoon vanilla essence
2 cups Edmonds standard grade flour
1 teaspoon Edmonds baking powder
1 teaspoon Edmonds baking soda
    dissolved in ¾ cup warm milk
½ cup (125 g) sour cream

To make the topping, combine all ingredients in a bowl. Mix well. To make the cake, cream butter and sugar until light and fluffy. Add eggs one at a time, beating well after each addition. Beat in vanilla essence. Sift flour and baking powder. Fold flour, milk and sour cream alternately into creamed mixture. Spoon into a greased 22 cm round cake tin that has the base lined with baking paper. Spoon topping evenly over cake, then gently press onto surface. Bake at 180°C for 1 hour or until a skewer inserted in centre of cake comes out clean. Leave in tin for 10 minutes before transferring to a wire rack to cool.

ORANGE CAKE ❧ 18

20 ❧ RHUBARB AND PECAN CRUST CAKE

SPICED FEIJOA CAKE ❧ 24

24 ❧ TENNIS CAKE

SEMOLINA CAKE

3 tablespoons Edmonds standard
  grade flour
½ cup semolina
4 eggs
½ cup sugar
1 tablespoon grated lemon zest

SYRUP
1 cup sugar
½ cup water
¼ cup lemon juice
1 teaspoon grated lemon zest

In a bowl, combine flour and semolina. Separate the eggs. Beat egg yolks and sugar together until pale and thick. Gently fold semolina mixture and lemon zest into egg mixture. Beat egg whites until stiff but not dry. Fold a quarter of egg whites into egg mixture, then remaining egg whites. Pour mixture into a 20 cm springform tin lined with baking paper. Bake at 180°C for 40 minutes or until skewer comes out clean when tested. Leave in tin 10 minutes before transferring to a serving plate. Pour hot syrup over cake about a quarter at a time, leaving time for the cake to soak up syrup.

SYRUP
Place sugar, water, lemon juice and zest in a small saucepan. Heat gently, stirring constantly until sugar has dissolved.

SIMNEL CAKE

500 g marzipan
icing sugar
250 g butter, softened
1 cup sugar
4 eggs
2½ cups Edmonds standard grade flour
1 teaspoon Edmonds baking powder
1½ cups sultanas
1½ cups currants
½ cup mixed peel
½ cup chopped glacé cherries

Cut marzipan into thirds. Using two of the marzipan pieces, roll out two rounds on greaseproof paper dusted with icing sugar to fit a 22 cm round cake tin. Cream butter and sugar until light and fluffy. Beat in eggs one at a time, beating well after each addition. Sift flour and baking powder together. Mix in sultanas, currants, peel and cherries. Fold into creamed mixture. Spoon half the mixture into the cake tin lined with baking paper, spreading the mixture evenly. Cover with one of the marzipan rounds, then spread remaining cake mixture on top and smooth. Bake at 150°C for 2 hours. Reduce heat to 130°C and bake for a further ½–1 hour or until an inserted skewer comes out clean. While cake is cooking, use the unrolled marzipan to make 11 balls. Place the second marzipan round on top of the hot cake and decorate with the 11 balls. Return the cake to the oven for about 15 minutes until the marzipan is lightly browned. Leave to cool in tin.

SPICED FEIJOA CAKE

175 g butter, softened
1 cup caster sugar
3 eggs
1 teaspoon vanilla essence
1 cup chopped peeled feijoa
¼ cup chopped crystallised ginger
2½ cups Edmonds standard grade flour
2 teaspoons Edmonds baking powder
½ teaspoon Edmonds baking soda
2 teaspoons ground ginger
1 cup (250 g) sour cream
Cream Cheese Icing (see page 223)
chopped crystallised ginger to garnish

Cream butter and sugar until light and fluffy. Add eggs one at a time, beating well after each addition. Beat in vanilla essence. Fold in feijoas and crystallised ginger. Sift together flour, baking powder, baking soda and ground ginger. Fold into creamed mixture. Fold in sour cream. Transfer mixture to a 22 cm round cake tin that has the base lined with baking paper. Bake at 180°C for 1 hour or until cake springs back when lightly pressed. Leave in tin for 10 minutes before transferring to a wire rack. When cake is cold, spread with Cream Cheese Icing. Garnish with crystallised ginger.

SULTANA CAKE

2 cups sultanas
water
250 g butter, chopped in small pieces
1 cup sugar
3 eggs, beaten
½ teaspoon lemon essence or almond
   essence
3 cups Edmonds standard grade flour
1½ teaspoons Edmonds baking powder

Put sultanas in a saucepan. Cover with water. Bring to the boil then simmer for 15 minutes. Drain thoroughly. Add butter. In a bowl, beat sugar into eggs until well combined. Add sultana mixture and essence. Sift flour and baking powder together. Mix sifted ingredients into fruit mixture. Spoon mixture into a 20 cm square cake tin lined with baking paper. Bake at 160°C for 1¼–1½ hours or until cake springs back when lightly touched. Leave in tin for 10 minutes before turning out onto a wire rack.

TENNIS CAKE

175 g butter, softened
1½ cups sugar
½ teaspoon vanilla essence
½ teaspoon almond essence
2 cups Edmonds standard grade flour
¼ teaspoon cinnamon
1 teaspoon Edmonds baking powder
4 eggs, beaten
¾ cup raisins
½ cup chopped glacé cherries
2 teaspoons grated lemon zest
2 tablespoons lemon juice

Cream butter and sugar until light and fluffy. Add vanilla and almond essences. Sift flour, cinnamon and baking powder together. Add eggs alternately with sifted dry ingredients. Mix in raisins, cherries, lemon zest and juice. Spoon mixture into a 22 cm round cake tin lined on the base with baking paper. Bake at 160°C for 1–1½ hours or until an inserted skewer comes out clean when tested. Leave in tin for 10 minutes before turning out onto a wire rack.

BISCUITS

AFGHANS

200 g butter, softened
½ cup sugar
1¼ cups Edmonds standard grade flour
3 tablespoons cocoa
1½ cups cornflakes
Chocolate Icing (see page 223)
walnuts (optional)

Cream butter and sugar until light and fluffy. Sift flour and cocoa. Stir into creamed mixture. Fold in cornflakes. Spoon mounds of mixture onto a greased oven tray, gently pressing the mixture together. Bake at 180°C for 15 minutes or until set. When cold, ice with Chocolate Icing and decorate with a walnut if wished.

ALMOND BISCUITS

125 g butter, softened
½ cup sugar
1 egg
½ teaspoon almond essence
1½ cups Edmonds standard grade flour
1 teaspoon Edmonds baking powder
18 blanched almonds, halved

Cream butter and sugar until light and fluffy. Add egg and almond essence, beating well. Sift in flour and baking powder. Mix to a firm dough. Roll into small balls. Place on a greased oven tray. Press half a blanched almond on each. Bake at 180°C for 15 minutes or until cooked.

ALMOND CRESCENT BISCUITS

200 g butter, softened
½ cup caster sugar
½ teaspoon almond essence
1¼ cups Edmonds standard grade flour
70 g packet ground almonds
icing sugar to dust

Cream butter and sugar until light and fluffy. Beat in almond essence. Sift flour. Fold flour and ground almonds into creamed mixture. Spoon mixture into a piping bag fitted with a 1 cm round star nozzle. Pipe small crescent shapes onto lightly greased oven trays. Bake at 160°C for 25 minutes. Cool biscuits on trays. Five minutes after removing from the oven, dust biscuits lightly with icing sugar.

ALMOND SHORTBREAD RINGS

250 g butter, softened
1 cup icing sugar
3–4 drops almond essence
1½ cups Edmonds standard grade flour
¾ cup Edmonds Fielder's cornflour
70 g packet ground almonds

Cream butter and icing sugar until light and fluffy. Add almond essence. Sift flour and cornflour. Stir into butter mixture along with ground almonds, mixing to a soft dough. Transfer dough to a lightly floured surface. Knead lightly for 2 minutes. Divide dough in half. Shape each portion into a ball and place in the centre of lightly greased oven trays. Flatten each ball into a circle about 20 cm in diameter. Using a sharp knife or pizza wheel, divide rounds into eight equal portions, cutting almost right through the dough. Prick each section several times with a fork. Bake at 150°C for 40 minutes. Cool on a wire rack. To divide shortbread, break into sections along the marked lines.

ANZAC BISCUITS

½ cup Edmonds standard grade flour
½ cup sugar
¾ cup coconut
¾ cup rolled oats
75 g butter
1 tablespoon golden syrup
½ teaspoon Edmonds baking soda
2 tablespoons boiling water

Mix together flour, sugar, coconut and rolled oats. Melt butter and golden syrup. Dissolve baking soda in the boiling water and add to butter and golden syrup. Stir butter mixture into the dry ingredients. Place level tablespoons of mixture onto cold greased trays. Press out with a fork. Bake at 180°C for about 15 minutes or until golden.

ALMOND CRESCENT BISCUITS ◈ 27

28 ◈ ALMOND SHORTBREAD RINGS

BELGIUM BISCUITS ◈ 30

30 ◈ BISCOTTI

BELGIUM BISCUITS

MAKES 18

125 g butter, softened
¼ cup brown sugar
1 egg
2 cups Edmonds standard grade flour
1 teaspoon Edmonds baking powder
1 teaspoon cinnamon
1 teaspoon ground ginger
1 teaspoon mixed spice
1 teaspoon cocoa

ICING
¾–1 cup icing sugar
¼ teaspoon raspberry or vanilla
    essence
few drops red food colouring
water

FILLING
½ cup raspberry jam, approximately

Cream butter and sugar until light and fluffy. Add egg and beat well. Sift flour, baking powder, cinnamon, ginger, mixed spice and cocoa together. Mix into creamed mixture to make a firm dough. On a lightly floured board, roll dough out to 3 mm thickness. Cut out rounds using a 6.5 cm cutter. Arrange on greased oven tray and bake at 180°C for 15 minutes or until golden. When cold, ice half the biscuits. Spread the un-iced biscuits with raspberry jam and place iced biscuits on top.

ICING
Mix icing sugar with essence and colouring. Add sufficient water to make a pink spreadable icing.

BISCOTTI

MAKES APPROX 40

2 cups Edmonds standard grade flour
2 teaspoons Edmonds baking powder
pinch of salt
½ cup caster sugar
1 teaspoon almond essence
3 eggs
½ cup chopped, toasted almonds

Sift flour, baking powder and salt into a bowl. Mix in caster sugar. Lightly beat almond essence and eggs together. Mix into dry ingredients with almonds until well combined. The dough should be firm. Add more flour if necessary. Shape into a log about 30 cm long. Place on a greased oven tray and flatten the log with the palm of your hand. Bake at 180°C for 35 minutes or until cooked. Cool then cut log into 1 cm slices on the diagonal. Place slices on an oven tray. Bake at 150°C for 10 minutes or until biscotti are dry and crisp. Store in an airtight container.

BRANDY SNAPS

1 teaspoon ground ginger
3 tablespoons golden syrup
½ cup sugar
75 g butter
½ cup Edmonds standard grade flour
whipped cream, to fill

Put ginger, golden syrup, sugar and butter in a saucepan. Heat gently until butter has melted, stirring occasionally. Remove from heat and allow to cool slightly. Sift flour into saucepan. Stir to combine. Drop tablespoons of mixture onto a greased oven tray, no more than four at a time. Allow room for spreading. Bake at 180°C for 8 minutes or until golden. Cool slightly until able to be removed from tray without collapsing. Remove hot brandy snaps with a spatula and wrap around the handle of wooden spoon to shape. You will probably fit two on one handle. Cool slightly and slide off. Leave until set. Fill with whipped cream.

CHOCOLATE BROWNIE BISCUITS

150 g dark chocolate, chopped
125 g butter, chopped
2 eggs
¾ cup caster sugar
2 teaspoons vanilla essence
1¼ cups Edmonds standard grade flour
¼ cup cocoa
¼ teaspoon Edmonds baking powder
½ cup chopped walnuts

Combine chocolate and butter in a saucepan. Stir constantly over a low heat until melted and smooth. Using an electric mixer, beat eggs, sugar and vanilla essence until thick and pale. Sift together flour, cocoa and baking powder. Fold chocolate mixture into egg mixture. Fold in dry ingredients and walnuts. Drop tablespoons of mixture onto greased oven trays. Bake at 180°C for 12 minutes. Transfer to wire racks to cool.

CHOCOLATE CHIP BISCUITS

125 g butter, softened
¼ cup sugar
3 tablespoons sweetened condensed milk
few drops vanilla essence
1½ cups Edmonds standard grade flour
1 teaspoon Edmonds baking powder
½ cup chocolate chips

Cream butter, sugar, condensed milk and vanilla essence until light and fluffy. Sift flour and baking powder together. Mix sifted dry ingredients and chocolate chips into creamed mixture. Roll tablespoons of mixture into balls. Place on a greased oven tray and flatten with a floured fork. Bake at 180°C for 20 minutes.

COFFEE KISSES

250 g butter, softened
¾ cup icing sugar
3 teaspoons instant coffee powder
2 teaspoons milk
2 cups Edmonds standard grade flour
½ cup Edmonds Fielder's cornflour

COFFEE ICING

1 cup icing sugar
1 teaspoon instant coffee powder
2 teaspoons melted butter
milk to mix

Cream butter and icing sugar until light and fluffy. Dissolve coffee powder in milk. Add to creamed mixture and beat well. Sift flour and cornflour. Stir into creamed mixture. Spoon mixture into a piping bag fitted with a 2 cm round star nozzle. Pipe 4 cm round rosettes onto greased oven trays, allowing a little room for spreading. Bake at 180°C for 15–18 minutes. Cool on oven trays. Sandwich biscuits together with Coffee Icing. To make the icing, combine icing sugar and coffee in a bowl. Stir in butter and sufficient milk to mix to a spreadable consistency.

DUSKIES

125 g butter, softened
1 cup icing sugar
1 egg
1¼ cups Edmonds standard grade flour
2 tablespoons cocoa
1 teaspoon Edmonds baking powder
½ cup desiccated coconut
½ cup chopped walnuts
Chocolate Icing (see page 223)
desiccated coconut to sprinkle

Cream butter and sugar, add egg then beat. Sift in flour, cocoa and baking powder. Add coconut and walnuts. Mix and place in small spoonfuls on cold, greased trays. Bake at 200°C for 12–15 minutes. When cold, ice with Chocolate Icing and decorate with desiccated coconut.

BRANDY SNAPS ⧫ 31

31 ⧫ CHOCOLATE CHIP BISCUITS

COFFEE KISSES ⧫ 32

32 ⧫ DUSKIES

ESPRESSO BISCUITS WITH FUDGE FILLING

200 g butter, softened
¾ cup icing sugar
2 teaspoons instant espresso coffee
   powder
1 teaspoon hot water
1½ cups Edmonds standard grade flour
¾ cup Edmonds Fielder's cornflour
½ teaspoon Edmonds baking powder

FUDGE FILLING
100 g dark chocolate, chopped
3 tablespoons butter
3 tablespoons icing sugar

Cream butter and icing sugar until light and fluffy. Dissolve coffee in the water. Add to creamed mixture and beat well. Sift flour, cornflour and baking powder. Add to creamed mixture. Mix well. Roll dough into small balls (the size of large marbles) and place on greased oven trays. Flatten slightly with the palm of your hand. Bake at 180°C for 20 minutes. Cool on wire racks. To make the Fudge Filling, combine chocolate and butter in a small saucepan. Stir constantly over a low heat until melted and smooth. Add icing sugar. Mix well. Sandwich two biscuits together with Fudge Filling.

FLORENTINES

125 g butter, softened
½ cup sugar
5 tablespoons golden syrup
¼ cup Edmonds standard grade flour
70 g packet sliced almonds
½ cup chopped glacé cherries
½ cup chopped walnuts
¼ cup chopped mixed peel

ICING
150 g cooking chocolate

Cream butter and sugar. Beat in golden syrup. Sift in flour. Add almonds, cherries, walnuts and peel. Mix well. Place tablespoons of mixture on trays lined with baking paper, spacing them well apart to allow for spreading. Cook four at a time. Press each one out as flat and round as possible, using a knife. Bake at 180°C for 10 minutes or until golden brown. Remove from oven and leave on tray for 5 minutes before transferring to a wire rack. To make icing, melt cooking chocolate in a bowl over hot water. When biscuits are cold, ice with chocolate on the flat side of biscuit.

GINGER BISCUITS

200 g butter, softened
¾ cup caster sugar
¼ cup golden syrup
2¼ cups Edmonds standard grade flour
2 teaspoons Edmonds baking soda
1 tablespoon ground ginger

Cream butter and caster sugar until light and fluffy. Add golden syrup and beat well. Sift dry ingredients. Stir into creamed mixture to form a soft dough. Roll heaped teaspoons of mixture into balls. Place 3–4 cm apart on greased oven trays. Flatten slightly with the palm of your hand. Bake at 160°C for 30 minutes. Cool on wire racks.

HAZELNUT SHORTBREAD FINGERS

MAKES 40

250 g butter, softened
1 cup icing sugar
1 cup Edmonds Fielder's cornflour
1¾ cups Edmonds standard grade flour
½ cup chopped roasted hazelnuts
melted dark chocolate for dipping
  shortbread (optional)

Cream butter and icing sugar until light and fluffy. Sift together cornflour and flour. Mix sifted ingredients and hazelnuts into creamed mixture. Knead well. Divide dough into equal halves and form into logs 6 cm across and 2 cm in depth. Cover with plastic wrap and refrigerate for 45 minutes. Using a serrated knife, cut 1 cm thick slices from the log. Place on greased oven trays. Prick with a fork. Bake at 160°C for 35–40 minutes or until pale golden. If desired, dip each shortbread finger into melted dark chocolate to cover half the shortbread.

HOKEY POKEY BISCUITS

MAKES 22

125 g butter
½ cup sugar
1 tablespoon golden syrup
1 tablespoon milk
1½ cups Edmonds standard grade flour
1 teaspoon Edmonds baking soda

Combine butter, sugar, golden syrup and milk in a saucepan. Heat until butter is melted and mixture nearly boiling, stirring constantly. Remove from heat and allow mixture to cool to lukewarm. Sift flour and baking soda together. Add to the cooled mixture. Stir well. Roll tablespoons of mixture into balls and place on ungreased oven trays. Flatten with a floured fork. Bake at 180°C for 15–20 minutes or until golden brown.

MACADAMIA NUT AND WHITE CHOCOLATE BISCUITS

MAKES 40

200 g butter, softened
1 cup caster sugar
2 eggs
1 teaspoon vanilla essence
3 cups Edmonds standard grade flour
2 teaspoons Edmonds baking powder
100 g chopped white chocolate
⅓ cup chopped macadamia nuts

Cream butter and caster sugar until light and fluffy. Add eggs one at a time, beating well after each addition. Beat in vanilla essence. Sift flour and baking powder. Stir into creamed mixture along with chocolate and nuts. Take heaped teaspoons of mixture and roll into balls. Place on greased oven trays, allowing room for spreading. Flatten slightly with a floured fork. Bake at 180°C for 15–18 minutes until golden. Cool on wire racks.

MELTING MOMENTS » 38

38 » MERINGUES

OAT BISCUITS » 38

40 » ORANGE MELTING MOMENTS

MELTING MOMENTS

MAKES 16

200 g butter, softened
¾ cup icing sugar
1 cup Edmonds standard grade flour
1 cup Edmonds Fielder's cornflour
½ teaspoon Edmonds baking powder
Butter Icing (see page 223) or
   raspberry jam

Cream butter and icing sugar until light and fluffy. Sift flour, cornflour and baking powder together. Add to creamed mixture, mixing well. Roll dough into small balls the size of large marbles and place on a greased oven tray. Flatten slightly with a floured fork. Bake at 180°C for 20 minutes or until cooked. Cool and sandwich two biscuits together with Butter Icing or raspberry jam.

MERINGUES

MAKES 12

2 egg whites
½ cup sugar
whipped cream

Beat egg whites until stiff but not dry. Add half the sugar and beat well. Repeat with remaining sugar. Beat until thick and glossy. Pipe or spoon small amounts of meringue onto a greased oven tray. Bake at 120°C for 1–1½ hours or until the meringues are dry but not brown. Cool and when required to serve, sandwich meringues together in pairs with whipped cream. Store unfilled meringues in an airtight container.

OAT BISCUITS

MAKES 30

125 g butter, softened
½ cup sugar
2 tablespoons honey
1 cup Edmonds standard grade flour
1 teaspoon Edmonds baking powder
½ teaspoon cinnamon
1½ cups rolled oats

Cream butter, sugar and honey together until pale. Sift flour, baking powder and cinnamon together. Add sifted dry ingredients and rolled oats to creamed mixture, stirring well. Roll tablespoons of mixture into balls. Place on a greased oven tray. Flatten with a floured fork and bake at 180°C for 15 minutes or until golden. Transfer to a wire rack to cool.

PEANUT BROWNIES ⬧ 40

40 ⬧ SHORTBREAD

YOGHURT RAISIN BISCUITS ⬧ 41

41 ⬧ YOYOS

ORANGE MELTING MOMENTS

MAKES 22

200 g butter, softened
¾ cup icing sugar
finely grated zest of 1 medium orange
1 cup Edmonds standard grade flour
1 cup Edmonds Fielder's cornflour
½ teaspoon Edmonds baking powder

ORANGE ICING
1 cup icing sugar
1 teaspoon butter
1 tablespoon freshly squeezed orange juice
a little boiling water to mix

Cream butter and icing sugar until light and fluffy. Beat in orange zest. Sift flour, cornflour and baking powder. Add to creamed mixture. Mix well. Roll dough into small balls (the size of large marbles) and place on a greased oven tray. Flatten slightly with a floured fork. Bake at 180°C for 20 minutes. Cool on wire racks. To make the Orange Icing, place icing sugar, butter and orange juice in a bowl. Add sufficient water to mix to a spreadable consistency. Sandwich two biscuits together with Orange Icing.

PEANUT BROWNIES

MAKES 20

125 g butter, softened
1 cup sugar
1 egg
1½ cups Edmonds standard grade flour
1 teaspoon Edmonds baking powder
pinch of salt
2 tablespoons cocoa
1 cup peanuts, roasted and husked

Cream butter and sugar until light and fluffy. Add egg and beat well. Sift flour, baking powder, salt and cocoa together. Mix into creamed mixture. Add cold peanuts and mix well. Roll tablespoons of mixture into balls. Place on greased oven trays. Flatten with a floured fork. Bake at 180°C for 15 minutes or until cooked.

SHORTBREAD

MAKES 24

250 g butter, softened
1 cup icing sugar
1 cup Edmonds Fielder's cornflour
2 cups Edmonds standard grade flour
¼ teaspoon salt

Cream butter and icing sugar until light and fluffy. Add sifted cornflour, flour and salt to creamed mixture. Knead mixture and form into a long loaf measuring 5 cm across and 2 cm in depth. Cover with plastic wrap and place in refrigerator. When required, cut into 1.5 cm thick slices or less and place on a cold greased baking tray. Bake at 180°C for 15–20 minutes.

YOGHURT RAISIN BISCUITS

125 g butter
½ cup sugar
1 egg
1 teaspoon vanilla essence
¾ cup yoghurt-covered raisins
2 cups Edmonds standard grade flour
1½ teaspoons Edmonds baking powder

Melt butter. Cool slightly. Using a wooden spoon, beat sugar and egg together for 2 minutes, until thick and pale. Add butter and mix well. Stir in vanilla essence and raisins. Sift flour and baking powder. Stir into liquid ingredients. Take heaped teaspoons of mixture and form into balls. Place 3–4 cm apart on greased oven trays. Flatten slightly with the palm of your hand. Bake at 180°C for 15 minutes until golden. Cool on wire racks.

YOYOS

175 g butter, softened
¼ cup icing sugar
few drops vanilla essence
1½ cups Edmonds standard grade flour
¼ cup Edmonds custard powder

BUTTER FILLING
75 g butter, softened
¾ cup icing sugar
3 tablespoons Edmonds custard
   powder

Cream butter and icing sugar until light and fluffy. Add vanilla essence. Sift flour and custard powder together. Mix sifted ingredients into creamed mixture. Roll teaspoons of mixture into balls. Place on a greased oven tray. Flatten with a floured fork. Bake at 180°C for 15–20 minutes. To make butter filling, beat all ingredients together until well combined. When Yoyos are cold, sandwich pairs together with butter filling.

SLICES

APPLE SHORTCAKE SQUARES

4 apples, peeled and sliced
finely grated zest and juice of ½ a
   lemon
1 tablespoon sugar
2 tablespoons water
2 cups Edmonds standard grade flour
1 teaspoon Edmonds baking powder
125 g butter
¼ cup sugar
1 egg, beaten
1–2 tablespoons milk
icing sugar to dust

Put apples, lemon zest and juice, first measure of sugar and water in saucepan and cook slowly until apples are soft. Sift flour and baking powder into a bowl. Cut in butter until it resembles coarse breadcrumbs. Mix in second measure of sugar and egg. Add sufficient milk to mix to a soft dough. Knead until smooth. Form into a ball and wrap in plastic wrap. Refrigerate for 30 minutes. Divide dough in half and roll out each piece to fit a greased 22 cm square cake tin. Place one piece of dough in tin and spread apple over it. Lightly press remaining dough on top. Bake at 180°C for 25 minutes. Cool. Dust with sifted icing sugar. Cut into squares.

APRICOT AND PISTACHIO NUT SLICE

FILLING
400 g roughly chopped dried apricots
1 cup water
½ cup sugar
finely grated zest of 1 lemon
½ cup roughly chopped pistachio nuts

OAT CRUMBLE
200 g butter, softened
1 cup lightly packed brown sugar
2 cups Edmonds standard grade flour
1 teaspoon Edmonds baking powder
1 teaspoon ground ginger
2 cups rolled oats

To make the filling, place apricots, water, sugar and lemon zest in a saucepan. Cook over a low heat for about 15 minutes until all the liquid is absorbed and the apricots are soft. Remove from heat. Cool. Stir in nuts. For the oat crumble base, cream butter and sugar until light and fluffy. Sift together flour, baking powder and ginger. Add to creamed mixture, along with the rolled oats. Mix well. Press three-quarters of the oat crumble over the base of a greased 20 × 30 cm shallow baking tin that has the base lined with baking paper. Spread apricot filling over the base, then sprinkle remaining oat mixture over top. Use the back of a spoon to lightly press topping into filling. Bake at 180°C for 40 minutes until golden. Cool in tin before cutting.

CARAMEL DATE FINGERS

FILLING
1 cup pitted dates, chopped
1 cup water
1 tablespoon brown sugar
1 teaspoon butter
2 teaspoons cocoa
¼ teaspoon vanilla essence

BASE
125 g butter
½ cup sugar
1 egg
1¾ cups Edmonds standard grade flour
1 teaspoon Edmonds baking powder

To make the filling, combine dates, water, sugar, butter and cocoa in a saucepan. Cook gently over a low heat, stirring frequently, until a paste-like consistency is obtained. Add vanilla essence. Cool. For the base, cream butter and sugar until light and fluffy. Add egg and beat well. Sift flour and baking powder together. Stir into creamed mixture. Press out half the mixture to fit the base of a greased 20 cm square tin. Spread with date mixture. Crumble remaining base mixture over filling. Press lightly with the back of a spoon. Bake at 180°C for 30 minutes or until golden. Cut into fingers.

NOTE: Other dried fruits such as prunes, apricots and raisins, alone or mixed, can replace dates.

CARAMEL SLICE

150 g butter
1 tablespoon golden syrup
½ cup brown sugar
1 cup Edmonds standard grade flour
1 teaspoon Edmonds baking powder
1 cup rolled oats

CARAMEL ICING
1 cup brown sugar
2 tablespoons condensed milk
2 tablespoons butter
1 cup icing sugar
1 tablespoon hot water

Chocolate Icing (see page 223)

Melt butter, golden syrup and brown sugar in a saucepan large enough to mix all the ingredients. Mix in flour, baking powder and rolled oats until combined. Press into a shallow 20 cm square tin lined on the base with baking paper. Bake at 180°C for 15 minutes. Spread with warm Caramel Icing and top with Chocolate Icing. Cut into squares or fingers.

CARAMEL ICING
Combine brown sugar, condensed milk and butter in a saucepan. Heat until bubbling and remove from heat. Add icing sugar and water. Beat to combine.

CHINESE CHEWS

2 eggs
1 cup brown sugar
75 g butter, melted
1 teaspoon vanilla essence
1½ cups Edmonds standard grade flour
1 teaspoon Edmonds baking powder
pinch of salt
½ cup rolled oats
¾ cup chopped dates
¾ cup chopped walnuts
¾ cup crystallised ginger

Beat eggs and sugar until well mixed. Add butter and vanilla essence. Into a large bowl, sift flour, baking powder and salt. Stir in rolled oats. Pour egg mixture into the sifted dry ingredients. Add dates, walnuts and ginger. Mix well. Spread mixture into a 23 cm square cake tin lined with baking paper. Bake at 180°C for 30–35 minutes or until cooked. Cut into squares while still hot.

COCONUT AND ALMOND SLICE

250 g packet plain sweet biscuits, crushed
¾ cup chopped toasted blanched almonds
1 cup coconut
finely grated zest and juice of 1 lemon
2 drops almond essence
100 g butter
½ cup sweetened condensed milk

LEMON ICING
1½ cups icing sugar
2 tablespoons butter
1 teaspoon lemon juice
boiling water to mix

Combine biscuit crumbs, almonds, coconut, lemon zest, juice and almond essence in a bowl. Place butter and condensed milk in a small saucepan. Stir over a low heat until the butter melts. Pour over biscuit mixture. Mix well. Press over the base of a 20 × 25 cm shallow baking dish. Refrigerate for 1 hour until firm. To make the icing, combine all ingredients in a bowl, adding sufficient boiling water to mix to a stiff paste. Spread over slice. Refrigerate for 1 hour or until set. Cut into fingers. Store in the refrigerator.

COCONUT CHOCOLATE BROWNIES

125 g butter
¼ cup cocoa
1 cup sugar
2 eggs
1 teaspoon vanilla essence
½ cup coconut
½ cup Edmonds standard grade flour
½ teaspoon Edmonds baking powder
icing sugar to dust

Melt butter in a medium-sized saucepan. Add cocoa. Stir over a low heat for 1 minute. Remove from heat. Stir in sugar. Add eggs one at a time, beating well after each addition. Beat in vanilla essence and coconut. Sift flour and baking powder. Stir into mixture. Pour into a greased and lined shallow 20 cm square cake tin. Bake at 180°C for 30–35 minutes. Leave in tin for 5 minutes before turning out onto a wire rack. Cut into bars when cold. Dust with icing sugar.

COCONUT DREAM

125 g butter, softened
½ cup brown sugar
1½ cups Edmonds standard grade flour
1 teaspoon Edmonds baking powder

TOPPING
2 eggs
1 cup brown sugar
4 teaspoons Edmonds standard grade
    flour
½ teaspoon Edmonds baking powder
1 teaspoon vanilla essence
1½ cups coconut
1 cup chopped nuts

Cream butter and sugar until light and fluffy. Sift flour and baking powder together. Mix into creamed mixture. Press into a 20 × 30 cm sponge roll tin lined with baking paper. Bake at 200°C for 8 minutes. Pour topping mixture over cooked base. Bake at 160°C for 40–45 minutes or until brown. Cut into squares.

TOPPING
Beat eggs. Add sugar and beat until thick. Sift flour and baking powder together. Fold into egg mixture. Stir in vanilla essence, coconut and nuts.

COFFEE OAT SLICE

BASE
175 g butter, softened
½ cup caster sugar
1¾ cups Edmonds standard grade flour

COFFEE FILLING
395 g can sweetened condensed milk
50 g butter
3 teaspoons instant coffee powder

OAT TOPPING
1 cup rolled oats
1 cup coarse coconut
50 g butter, melted
2 tablespoons golden syrup

To make the base, cream butter and sugar until light and fluffy. Add flour. Mix to a soft dough. Press over the base of a greased 20 × 30 cm shallow baking tin that has the base lined with baking paper. Bake at 180°C for 15 minutes until light golden. Cool slightly. For the filling, place all ingredients in a small saucepan. Stir over a low heat until butter has melted and mixture is smooth. Bring to the boil, stirring constantly. Spread over partially cooked base. To make the topping, combine all ingredients in a bowl. Mix well. Sprinkle over coffee filling. Bake at 180°C for a further 15 minutes until golden. Cool in tin before cutting.

COFFEE WALNUT SLICE

BASE
175 g butter, softened
1 egg
2 cups Edmonds standard grade flour
½ cup caster sugar
¾ teaspoon Edmonds baking powder

FILLING
395 g can sweetened condensed milk
2 tablespoons butter
2 tablespoons golden syrup
2 teaspoons coffee and chicory
    essence
¾ cup roughly chopped walnuts

TOPPING
125 g butter, softened
½ cup caster sugar
1 cup Edmonds standard grade flour
1 teaspoon cinnamon

To make the base, beat butter, egg, flour, caster sugar and baking powder to a soft dough using an electric mixer. Press over the base of a greased shallow 25 cm square baking tin. Prick all over with a fork. Bake at 180°C for 20–25 minutes until golden. Next, prepare the filling. Place all filling ingredients in a saucepan. Stir over a low heat for 4–5 minutes until the mixture thickens. Remove from heat. Cool slightly. To make topping, beat all ingredients together for 1 minute with an electric mixer. Form into a ball and cover with plastic wrap. Refrigerate for at least 10 minutes. Spread cooled filling over cooked base. Coarsely grate topping dough over filling. Bake for 25–30 minutes until golden. Cool before cutting into slices.

DATE SHORTCAKE

1½ cups chopped dates
2 tablespoons water
3 tablespoons lemon juice
125 g butter, softened
½ cup sugar
1 egg
1 cup Edmonds standard grade flour
1 cup Edmonds Fielder's cornflour
1 teaspoon Edmonds baking powder
Lemon Icing (see page 223)

Put dates into a small saucepan, add water and lemon juice. Cook over a low heat until dates are soft. Cool. In a bowl, cream butter and sugar until light and fluffy. Add egg, then sifted flour, cornflour and baking powder. Knead. Roll out half the mixture and place on a cold greased tray. Spread date mixture on shortcake. Roll out other half of shortcake and place on top. Bake at 190°C for 25 minutes. When cold, ice with Lemon Icing. Cut into squares.

GINGER CRUNCH

125 g butter, softened
½ cup sugar
1½ cups Edmonds standard grade flour
1 teaspoon Edmonds baking powder
1 teaspoon ground ginger

GINGER ICING
75 g butter
¾ cup icing sugar
2 tablespoons golden syrup
3 teaspoons ground ginger

Cream butter and sugar until light and fluffy. Sift flour, baking powder and ginger together. Mix into creamed mixture. Turn dough out onto a lightly floured board. Knead well. Press dough into a 20 × 30 cm sponge roll tin lined with baking paper. Bake at 190°C for 20–25 minutes or until light brown. Pour hot Ginger Icing over base. Cut into squares while still warm.

GINGER ICING
In a small saucepan, combine butter, icing sugar, golden syrup and ginger. Heat until butter is melted, stirring constantly.

HONEY NUT BARS

BASE
1½ cups Edmonds standard grade flour
½ teaspoon Edmonds baking powder
¼ cup icing sugar
150 g butter, softened
2 egg yolks

TOPPING
75 g butter
⅓ cup liquid honey
⅓ cup sugar
¾ cup hazelnuts
½ cup each blanched almonds, walnut pieces, pecan nuts

To make the base, place flour, baking powder, icing sugar and butter in a food processor. Pulse until mixture is crumbly. Add egg yolks and pulse until mixture comes together. Press over the base of an 18 × 27 cm shallow baking tin lined with baking paper and greased. Prick several times with a fork. Bake at 180°C for 15 minutes. To make the topping, place butter, honey and sugar in a saucepan. Stir over a low heat until mixture boils. Simmer for 2 minutes. Remove from heat and stir in nuts. Spread warm topping evenly over base. Bake for 20 minutes at 180°C. Cool, then cut into bars. Refrigerate during warmer weather.

LEMON SLICE

150 g butter
1 cup Edmonds standard grade flour
½ cup icing sugar

TOPPING
2 tablespoons Edmonds custard powder
½ teaspoon Edmonds baking powder
1 cup sugar
½ cup lemon juice
1 tablespoon grated lemon zest
3 eggs

Melt the butter. Remove from heat and mix in flour and icing sugar. Press into the base of a 20 × 30 cm sponge roll tin lined with baking paper. Bake at 180°C for 15–20 minutes or until lightly golden. Pour over topping and bake for a further 25 minutes or until set. Cut into slices when cold.

TOPPING
Mix custard powder, baking powder, sugar, lemon juice, lemon zest and eggs together until combined.

LOUISE CAKE

150 g butter, softened
¼ cup sugar
4 eggs, separated
2½ cups Edmonds standard grade flour
2 teaspoons Edmonds baking powder
¼ cup raspberry jam
½ cup sugar
½ cup coconut

Cream butter and first measure of sugar until light and fluffy. Beat in egg yolks. Sift flour and baking powder together. Stir into creamed mixture. Press dough into a 20 × 30 cm sponge roll tin lined on the base with baking paper. Spread raspberry jam over the base. In a bowl, beat egg whites until stiff but not dry. Mix in the second measure of sugar and coconut. Spread this meringue mixture over jam. Bake at 180°C for 30 minutes or until meringue is dry and lightly coloured. Cut into squares while still warm.

NUTTY CRUNCH SLICE

1 cup sesame seeds
1 cup pumpkin kernels
1 cup coconut
1 cup chopped Brazil nuts
250 g packet Gingernut biscuits
½ cup chopped dried apricots
1 teaspoon ground ginger
125 g butter
½ cup sweetened condensed milk

Combine sesame seeds, pumpkin kernels, coconut and nuts in a frying pan. Stir continuously over a low–medium heat for 6–8 minutes until mixture starts to pop and the coconut turns a light golden colour. Transfer mixture to a bowl. Crush Gingernuts to a fine crumb in a food processor. Stir crumbs, apricots and ginger into toasted mixture. Place butter and condensed milk in a small saucepan. Stir over a low heat until butter has melted. Pour over dry ingredients and mix well. Press mixture over the base of a lightly greased 20 × 30 cm shallow baking tin. Cover and refrigerate for 1 hour before cutting. Cover again and store in the refrigerator.

OATY DATE BARS

FILLING
2 cups pitted, chopped dates
¼ cup water
¼ cup lemon juice

BASE
125 g butter, softened
¾ cup brown sugar
1 egg
1 tablespoon golden syrup
1 teaspoon vanilla essence
1¼ cups Edmonds wholemeal flour
1 teaspoon Edmonds baking powder
1 cup rolled oats
1 cup coconut

To make the filling, combine dates, water and lemon juice in a saucepan. Cook over a low heat, stirring frequently, until dates are soft and all the liquid is absorbed. Cool. To make the base, cream butter and sugar until light and fluffy. Add egg and beat well. Beat in golden syrup and vanilla essence. Add flour, baking powder, rolled oats and coconut to creamed mixture. Mix well. Divide dough into two equal portions. Press one portion over the base of a greased 20 × 30 cm shallow baking tin. Spread filling over top. Dot small pieces of other portion of dough over filling and carefully spread together to form a top layer. Bake at 180°C for 25–30 minutes, until golden. Cool before cutting into fingers.

ROCKY ROAD SLICE

1 cup Edmonds standard grade flour
½ teaspoon Edmonds baking powder
3 tablespoons cocoa
¾ cup caster sugar
¾ cup coconut
125 g butter, melted
1 egg

TOPPING
250 g dark chocolate, chopped
2 tablespoons Kremelta
25 marshmallows
½ cup toasted coconut (see page 230)
½ cup pistachio nuts (or chopped
    walnuts)

Sift flour, baking powder and cocoa into a bowl. Stir in caster sugar and coconut. Add butter and egg and mix well. Spread over the base of a greased 18 × 27 cm shallow baking tin. Bake at 180°C for 20–25 minutes. Cool for 15 minutes, then spread with topping. To make the topping, place chocolate and Kremelta in a heatproof bowl and set over a saucepan of simmering water. Stir continuously until chocolate and Kremelta have melted and the mixture is smooth. Set aside for 5 minutes to cool slightly. Add marshmallows, coconut and nuts to melted chocolate. Mix well. Allow topping to set before cutting into pieces.

NOTE: During warm weather, refrigerate slice for setting and keep in the refrigerator.

WHITE AND DARK CHOCOLATE BROWNIE SLICE

200 g butter, softened
1 cup sugar
3 eggs
½ cup cocoa
1 cup Edmonds standard grade flour
¼ teaspoon Edmonds baking powder
100 g white chocolate, roughly chopped
¾ cup (75 g) chopped walnuts
⅓ cup milk
icing sugar to dust

Cream butter and sugar until light and fluffy. Add eggs one at a time, beating well after each addition. Sift together cocoa, flour and baking powder. Fold dry ingredients, chocolate, walnuts and milk into creamed mixture. Transfer to a thoroughly greased 20 cm square shallow cake tin. Bake at 150°C for about 50 minutes — the brownies should be a little sticky. Cool before cutting into squares. Dust with icing sugar.

MUFFINS
SCONES
LOAVES *AND*
TARTLETS

BLUEBERRY MUFFINS

MAKES 12

3 cups Edmonds standard grade flour
5 teaspoons Edmonds baking powder
¼ cup sugar
50 g butter
3 eggs
1½ cups milk
2 cups blueberries
icing sugar

Sift flour and baking powder into a bowl. Mix in sugar. Melt butter. Lightly beat eggs and milk together. Make a well in the centre of the dry ingredients. Add butter, milk mixture and blueberries. Mix quickly until just combined. Three-quarters fill greased muffin tins with mixture. Bake at 200°C for 15 minutes or until muffins spring back when lightly touched. Serve warm, dusted with icing sugar.

BRAN MUFFINS

MAKES 12

2 cups Edmonds standard grade flour
2 teaspoons Edmonds baking powder
1 teaspoon salt
1 teaspoon mixed spice
3 cups bran flakes
½ cup brown sugar
2 eggs
2 teaspoons Edmonds baking soda
2 cups milk
2 tablespoons golden syrup
50 g butter
1 cup sultanas

Sift flour, baking powder, salt and mixed spice into a large bowl. Mix in bran flakes and brown sugar. Make a well in the centre of the dry ingredients. Lightly beat eggs. Dissolve baking soda in milk. Melt golden syrup and butter together. Make a well in the centre of the dry ingredients. Add eggs, milk mixture, melted ingredients and sultanas. Mix quickly until just combined. Three-quarters fill greased muffin tins with mixture. Bake at 220°C for 15 minutes or until muffins spring back when lightly touched.

FETA AND PARSLEY MUFFINS

MAKES 12

150 g butter
2 cups milk
2 eggs
3½ cups Edmonds standard grade flour
3 teaspoons Edmonds baking powder
¼ teaspoon cayenne pepper
100 g feta cheese, diced
1 cup grated tasty cheddar cheese
3 tablespoons chopped parsley

Combine butter and milk in a small saucepan. Stir over a low heat until butter has melted. Remove from heat. Set aside to cool slightly. Whisk in eggs. Sift flour, baking powder and cayenne into a bowl. Stir in cheeses and parsley. Add liquid ingredients, stirring until just combined. Do not overmix. Divide mixture between 12 greased deep muffin tins. Bake at 200°C for 20–25 minutes until risen and golden. Leave in tins for 5 minutes.

TINY CHEESE MUFFINS

50 g butter
¾ cup milk
1 egg
1½ cups Edmonds standard grade flour
1½ teaspoons Edmonds baking powder
¼ teaspoon salt
¾ cup grated tasty cheddar cheese
1 tablespoon chopped parsley
   (optional)

Place butter and milk in a small saucepan. Stir over a low heat until butter has melted. Remove from heat and cool for 5 minutes. Whisk in egg. Sift flour, baking powder and salt. Stir in cheese and parsley. Stir liquid ingredients into flour, mixing just until combined — do not overmix. Spoon mixture into 18 greased tiny muffin tins. Bake at 200°C for 12 minutes until risen and golden. Cool in tins for 5 minutes before removing.

NOTE: This mixture can also be cooked in 6 regular muffin tins. Bake for 15 minutes.

PIKELETS

1 cup Edmonds standard grade flour
1 teaspoon Edmonds baking powder
¼ teaspoon salt
1 egg
¼ cup sugar
¾ cup milk, approximately

Sift flour, baking powder and salt into a bowl. In another bowl, beat egg and sugar until thick. Add with milk to the sifted ingredients. Mix until just combined. Drop tablespoons of the mixture from the point of a spoon onto a hot greased griddle or non-stick frying pan. Turn pikelets over when bubbles start to burst on the top surface. Cook second side until golden.

BLUEBERRY MUFFINS ⦚ 55

55 ⦚ BRAN MUFFINS

TINY CHEESE MUFFINS ⦚ 56

56 ⦚ PIKELETS

SCONES ⟋ 59

59 ⟋ BLUEBERRY CREAM CHEESE LOAF

DATE LOAF ⟋ 60

60 ⟋ FRESH LEMON LOAF

SCONES

3 cups Edmonds standard grade flour
6 teaspoons Edmonds baking powder
¼ teaspoon salt
50 g butter
1¼ cups milk
milk to brush tops

Sift flour, baking powder and salt into a bowl. Cut butter in until mixture resembles fine breadcrumbs. Add milk and mix quickly to a soft dough with a knife. Lightly knead. Lightly dust an oven tray with flour. Press scone dough out onto tray. Cut into 12 even-sized pieces. Leave a 2 cm space between scones. Brush tops with extra milk. Bake at 220°C for 10 minutes or until golden brown.

CHEESE SCONES
Add ½ cup grated tasty cheddar cheese and a pinch of cayenne pepper to flour. Before baking, top each scone with a small amount of grated cheese.

DATE SCONES
Add ¾ cup chopped dates, 1 tablespoon sugar and ½ teaspoon cinnamon to flour. Before baking, sprinkle scones with mixture of cinnamon and sugar.

SULTANA SCONES
Add ½ cup sultanas to flour.

BLUEBERRY CREAM CHEESE LOAF

125 g butter, softened
100 g cream cheese, softened
1¼ cups sugar
3 eggs
1 teaspoon vanilla essence
2 teaspoons finely grated lemon zest
1½ cups Edmonds standard grade flour
1½ teaspoons Edmonds baking powder
1 cup blueberries (fresh or frozen)

Beat butter, cream cheese and sugar until light and creamy. Add eggs one at a time, beating well after each addition. Beat in vanilla essence and zest. Sift flour and baking powder. Fold into creamed mixture. Lightly fold in blueberries. Grease a 20 × 11 cm (base measurement) loaf tin. Line the base with baking paper. Transfer mixture to prepared tin. Bake at 180°C for about 1 hour or until a skewer inserted in the centre of the loaf comes out clean. Stand for 5 minutes before transferring to a wire rack to cool. Slice and serve with butter.

NOTE: If using frozen blueberries, do not allow them to thaw before use.

DATE LOAF

1 cup chopped dates
1 cup boiling water
1 teaspoon Edmonds baking soda
1 tablespoon butter
1 cup brown sugar
1 egg
1 cup chopped walnuts
¼ teaspoon vanilla essence
2 cups Edmonds standard grade flour
1 teaspoon Edmonds baking powder

Put dates, water, soda and butter into a bowl. Stir until butter has melted. Set aside for 1 hour. Beat sugar, egg, walnuts and vanilla essence into date mixture. Sift flour and baking powder into date mixture, stirring to just combine. Pour mixture into a 22 cm loaf tin lined with baking paper. Bake at 180°C for 50–60 minutes or until loaf springs back when lightly touched. Leave in tin for 10 minutes before turning out onto a wire rack.

APRICOT LOAF
Replace dates with apricots.

FRESH LEMON LOAF

125 g butter, softened
¾ cup sugar
1 teaspoon grated lemon zest
2 eggs
2 cups Edmonds self-raising flour
¼ teaspoon salt
½ cup milk
¼ cup chopped walnuts

GLAZE
¼ cup lemon juice
¼ cup sugar

Cream butter, sugar and lemon zest until light and fluffy. Add eggs one at a time, beating well after each addition. Sift flour and salt. Fold into creamed mixture alternately with milk. Fold in walnuts. Transfer to a greased and lined 22 cm loaf tin. Bake at 180°C for 45–50 minutes or until loaf springs back when lightly touched. While loaf is hot, pour over glaze. Cool in tin. To make the glaze, place lemon juice and sugar in a small saucepan. Stir over a low heat until sugar dissolves. Bring to the boil. Remove from heat. Cool.

FRUIT TARTLETS

Sweet Shortcrust Pastry (see page 224)
or 200 g Edmonds sweet short pastry

FILLING
3 tablespoons Edmonds custard
powder
1 cup milk
2 egg yolks
2 tablespoons sugar
2 tablespoons brandy
½ cup cream, whipped

TOPPING
fresh or tinned fruit (e.g. grapes,
melon, strawberries, kiwifruit),
diced or sliced

GLAZE
¼ cup apricot jam
2 teaspoons water

Roll the chilled pastry out on a lightly floured surface to a thickness of 4 mm. Using a 7 cm round fluted biscuit cutter, stamp circles from the dough. Line eighteen 7 cm round tartlet tins. Prick the bases of pastry cases. Refrigerate for 10 minutes, then freeze for 5 minutes. Bake at 180°C for 12–15 minutes until golden. Cool. To make filling, mix custard powder to a smooth paste with a little of the milk. Whisk in remaining milk, yolks and sugar. Cook over a low heat, stirring constantly until the mixture thickens. Do not allow to boil. Stir in the brandy. Cover the surface of filling directly with plastic wrap to prevent skin forming. Cool for 1 hour. Fold in cream. Spoon filling into the prepared tartlet cases. Arrange the fruit on top of the custard. To make the glaze, gently heat together jam and water. Sieve. Spoon or brush glaze over the fruit.

GINGERBREAD LOAF

2 cups Edmonds standard grade flour
pinch of salt
1 tablespoon ground ginger
1 tablespoon cinnamon
2 eggs
½ cup sugar
100 g butter
2 tablespoons golden syrup
1½ teaspoons Edmonds baking soda
¾ cup natural unsweetened yoghurt
½ cup sultanas

Sift flour, salt, ginger and cinnamon into a bowl. In a separate bowl, beat eggs and sugar until thick and pale. Melt together butter and golden syrup and cool slightly. Add to egg and sugar mixture. Fold in dry ingredients. In a small bowl, dissolve baking soda in the yoghurt. Stir into the loaf mixture with sultanas until well combined. Spoon into a greased and lined 22 cm loaf tin. Bake at 180°C for 45–50 minutes. Leave in tin for 10 minutes before turning out onto a wire rack.

FRUIT TARTLETS ⫽ 61

MINI PECAN TARTLETS

PASTRY
¾ cup Edmonds standard grade flour
50 g butter
2 tablespoons sugar
1 egg yolk

FILLING
¼ cup brown sugar
¼ cup golden syrup
¼ cup cream
2 eggs
¼ cup chopped pecan nuts

24 pecan nuts to garnish
icing sugar to dust

To make the pastry, sift flour. Cut in butter until it resembles fine breadcrumbs. Stir in sugar. Add egg yolk. Mix to a stiff dough. Chill for 30 minutes before using. Roll pastry out to a thickness of 3 mm. Using a 7 cm round biscuit cutter, stamp shapes from pastry. Use pastry to line 24 mini muffin tins. Place muffin tins in the freezer while preparing the filling. Combine brown sugar, golden syrup and cream in a small saucepan. Stir over a low heat for 1–2 minutes until mixture is smooth. Remove from heat. Stir in eggs and chopped pecan nuts. Half fill pastry cases with mixture. Place a nut on top of each tartlet. Bake at 180°C for 12–15 minutes until the filling is set and the tartlets are golden. Just before serving, dust with icing sugar.

TINY LEMON CURD TARTLETS

LEMON CURD FILLING
1 tablespoon finely grated lemon zest
¼ cup lemon juice
2 eggs, lightly beaten
50 g butter
¼ cup caster sugar

PASTRY
100 g butter, softened
¼ cup caster sugar
1 egg yolk
1 cup Edmonds standard grade flour

To make the Lemon Curd Filling, combine lemon zest and juice, eggs, butter and sugar in the top of a double boiler or in a heatproof bowl set over simmering water. Stir constantly until sugar dissolves and curd thickens. Remove from heat. Cover and cool. For the pastry, cream butter and sugar until light and fluffy. Add egg yolk and beat well. Stir in flour. Gather pastry into a ball and wrap in plastic wrap. Refrigerate for 20 minutes. Roll pastry out on a lightly floured surface to a thickness of 2–3 mm. Using a 7 cm round biscuit cutter, cut circles from pastry. Transfer to mini muffin tins. Prick bases with a fork. Freeze for 5 minutes. Bake at 180°C for 10 minutes until golden. Remove pastry cases from tins and cool on a wire rack. Just before serving, fill with Lemon Curd Filling.

BREAKFAST

BACON RASHERS

SERVES 4

bacon

Cut rind and fat from bacon using scissors. Cut rashers in half if long. Rub bacon fat over the base of a frying pan. Arrange bacon in a single layer over base of heated pan. Cook over a moderate heat for 4 minutes for regular bacon or 5 minutes for crisp bacon. Drain on absorbent paper.

BANANAS WITH MAPLE SYRUP

SERVES 4

4 bananas
½ cup maple syrup

Wash and dry unpeeled bananas. Place bananas in a dry frying pan and cook over a moderate heat for about 5 minutes, turning during cooking. Cut bananas lengthwise and partly peel back skin. Spoon over 1 tablespoon of maple syrup into each split banana. Serve with bacon and eggs.

BIRCHER MUESLI

MAKES ABOUT 5 CUPS

70 g packet blanched almonds, chopped
½ cup chopped Brazil nuts
½ cup sunflower seeds
3 cups rolled oats
1 teaspoon cinnamon
1 cup chopped dried apple
½ cup chopped dried apricots

Combine almonds, Brazil nuts and sunflower seeds in a roasting dish. Bake at 190°C for 5–6 minutes, turning once, until lightly toasted. Cool. Combine with remaining ingredients. Mix well. Store in an airtight container.

BREAKFAST MUSHROOMS

100 g brown button mushrooms
1 clove garlic
25 g butter
2 teaspoons Edmonds Fielder's
   cornflour
1 cup low-fat milk
1 tablespoon chopped parsley
3 slices wholemeal toast

Wipe mushrooms and cut in half if large. Crush, peel and finely chop garlic. Melt butter in a saucepan. Sauté garlic and mushrooms for 3 minutes. Mix cornflour to a paste with a little of the measured milk. Add remaining milk to mushrooms. Bring to the boil and stir in the cornflour paste. Stir until mixture boils and thickens. Mix in parsley. Toast bread and cut in half diagonally. Trim crusts if wished. Allow three toast triangles per serving. Spoon mushroom mixture over toast. Serve hot.

CHUNKY HONEY TOASTED MUESLI

3 cups wholegrain rolled oats
½ cup Elfin wheatgerm
½ cup thread coconut
½ cup roughly chopped hazelnuts
¼ cup liquid honey
¼ cup canola oil
½ cup chopped dried apricots or dried
   peaches

Combine oats, wheatgerm, coconut and hazelnuts in a roasting dish. Drizzle over honey and oil. Mix well. Bake at 190°C for 20 minutes or until golden, stirring every 4–5 minutes. Stir in apricots. Cool. Transfer to an airtight container. Serve with seasonal fresh fruit and/or yoghurt. This muesli is particularly delicious served with Greek yoghurt.

BIRCHER MUESLI ✻ 65

66 ✻ CHUNKY HONEY TOASTED MUESLI

EGGS BENEDICT ✻ 68

68 ✻ MUSHROOM AND BACON FRITTATA

EGGS BENEDICT

HOLLANDAISE SAUCE
50 g butter
1 tablespoon lemon juice
2 egg yolks
¼ cup cream
½ teaspoon dry mustard
¼ teaspoon salt

8 rashers rindless bacon
4 English muffins
8 eggs
freshly ground black pepper to garnish

To make the hollandaise, melt butter in a double boiler. Add lemon juice, egg yolks and cream. Cook, stirring constantly, until thick and smooth. Do not boil or sauce will curdle. Remove from heat. Add mustard and salt and beat until smooth. Grill bacon until beginning to crisp. Split muffins in half and toast. Meanwhile, pour 4–5 cm of water into a deep frying pan. Bring to the boil, then reduce heat to a simmer. Break eggs into the pan. Cook for 3 minutes or until cooked to your liking. Place 2 muffins on each serving plate. Top each muffin with a rasher of bacon and an egg. Drizzle with hollandaise. Garnish with a sprinkling of pepper. Serve immediately.

NOTE: Sliced ham can be substituted for the bacon. It does not require grilling. For smaller appetites, serve a half portion.

MUSHROOM AND BACON FRITTATA

1 tablespoon pure olive oil
4 rashers rindless bacon, chopped
200 g button mushrooms, sliced
1 teaspoon crushed garlic
½ cup cream
8 eggs, lightly beaten
½ cup freshly grated parmesan cheese
1 tablespoon wholegrain mustard
salt and freshly ground black pepper
   to serve
Turkish bread, toasted, to serve

Heat oil in a heavy-based frying pan. Cook bacon, mushrooms and garlic for 6–8 minutes until pan is dry. Combine bacon mixture, cream, eggs, parmesan, mustard and salt and pepper in a bowl. Grease a 23 cm round cake tin. Line base with baking paper. Pour in frittata mixture. Bake at 180°C for 30–35 minutes or until frittata mixture is set and golden. Stand for 10 minutes before turning out. Cut into wedges and serve warm accompanied by toasted Turkish bread.

SALADS

CHICKEN AND ASPARAGUS SALAD
WITH MUSTARD DRESSING

DRESSING

2 tablespoons extra virgin olive oil
2 tablespoons freshly squeezed
    orange juice
1 tablespoon chopped parsley
2 teaspoons wholegrain mustard
salt and freshly ground black pepper
    to season

SALAD

20 asparagus spears
100 g snowpeas
2 cups sliced cooked chicken meat
2 firm, ripe avocados, peeled and
    sliced
½ cup quality walnut pieces

To make the dressing, combine all ingredients. Mix well. To make the salad, snap woody ends off asparagus. Cook in a little boiling water for 3–4 minutes until just tender. Drain and cool under cold running water. Add snowpeas to boiling water. Bring back to the boil, then tip into a sieve. Cool under cold running water. Drain well. Combine salad ingredients in a bowl. Pour over dressing and toss gently. Serve with fresh bread.

CHICKEN CAESAR SALAD

4 single boneless skinless chicken
    breasts
¼ cup extra virgin olive oil
2 tablespoons lemon juice
freshly ground black pepper to season
2 cups stale bread cubes (French
    bread or toast sliced bread is ideal)
1 cos lettuce
12 anchovy fillets
shavings of parmesan cheese
Caesar Salad Dressing (see page 225)

Place chicken breasts between two sheets of plastic wrap. Beat lightly with a heavy object (e.g. a rolling pin) to flatten to an even thickness of about 1 cm. Place in a single layer in a shallow dish. Combine 2 tablespoons of the oil, lemon juice and pepper. Pour over chicken, turning to coat. Cover and refrigerate for 2–4 hours. Cook chicken under a preheated grill or on a barbecue for 4–5 minutes on each side until cooked through. Set aside to cool. To make croûtons, pour remaining oil into a frying pan. Heat pan. Add bread cubes and cook until golden, turning frequently. Remove from pan and drain on kitchen paper. Wash and dry lettuce leaves. Slice chicken into strips. Combine lettuce, chicken, anchovy fillets and parmesan cheese in a bowl. Pour over Caesar Salad Dressing. Toss to combine. Scatter over croûtons.

GREEK SALAD

1 green capsicum, seeded and sliced
1 small onion, sliced
3 tomatoes, quartered
1 diced cucumber
½ cup pitted black olives
100 g feta cheese, cubed

DRESSING
¼ cup extra virgin olive oil
1 clove garlic, crushed
2 tablespoons spiced vinegar
¼ teaspoon sugar

Arrange capsicum, onion, tomatoes and cucumber in a salad bowl. To make the dressing, place all ingredients in a screw-top jar and shake vigorously just before using. Pour dressing over the salad ingredients in the bowl and toss to coat. Decorate with olives and feta cheese.

GRILLED VEGETABLES WITH VINAIGRETTE

8 brown mushroom flats
1 red pepper
1 green pepper
4 courgettes
12 asparagus spears
extra virgin olive oil

VINAIGRETTE
1 clove garlic
¾ cup extra virgin olive oil
¼ cup white vinegar
1 teaspoon wholegrain mustard
¼ teaspoon salt
2 tablespoons chopped fresh herbs
   (e.g. chives, parsley or basil)

Wipe mushrooms. Cut peppers in half and remove core and seeds. Cut into quarters. Trim courgettes. Cut in half lengthwise. Snap woody ends from asparagus. Brush vegetables with oil and grill under a hot grill or over the barbecue until golden. Place on a serving platter and pour over vinaigrette. Serve warm or cold.

VINAIGRETTE
Crush and peel garlic. Shake oil, vinegar, mustard, salt, herbs and garlic together in a screw-top jar until combined.

LUNCHBOX PASTA SALAD

SERVES 4

SALAD
150 g dried pasta bows
12 cherry tomatoes, halved (or 4
    tomatoes, quartered)
1 green capsicum, seeded, cored and
    diced
100 g cheddar cheese, cut in small
    dice
½ cup toasted pine nuts (optional)

DRESSING
2 tablespoons extra virgin olive oil
2 tablespoons wine vinegar
2 tablespoons freshly squeezed
    orange juice
1 tablespoon chopped parsley
salt and freshly ground black pepper
    to season

Cook pasta according to packet instructions. Transfer to a sieve. Cool under cold running water, then drain thoroughly. Combine all salad ingredients in a large bowl. Pour over dressing and toss to combine. To make the dressing, place all ingredients in a jar. Secure the lid and shake vigorously. To include this salad in the lunchbox, transfer to a lidded container. Include a fork.

ORZO PASTA SALAD

SERVES 4

SALAD
300 g orzo pasta
50 g sliced salami, diced
½ cup pistachio nuts
¼ cup chopped sundried tomatoes
15 stuffed green olives, halved

DRESSING
¼ cup extra virgin olive oil
2 tablespoons wine vinegar
2 tablespoons freshly squeezed
    orange juice
1 tablespoon chopped basil
2 cloves garlic, crushed
salt and freshly ground black pepper
    to season

Cook the pasta in boiling water for 10 minutes until al dente. Tip into a sieve, then rinse under cold running water. Drain thoroughly. Combine all salad ingredients in a bowl. To make the dressing, combine all ingredients. Mix well. Pour dressing over and toss lightly to combine.

GREEK SALAD ⬦ 71

74 ⬦ RATATOUILLE
70 ⬦ GRILLED VEGETABLES WITH VINAIGRETTE

LUNCHBOX PASTA SALAD ⬦ 72

72 ⬦ ORZO PASTA SALAD

RATATOUILLE

¼ cup pure olive oil
6 medium tomatoes, blanched, skins
    removed and chopped
½ teaspoon salt
black pepper
¼ teaspoon sugar
1 large onion, sliced
2 cloves garlic, crushed
1 green pepper, sliced
250 g courgettes, sliced
1 eggplant, chopped

Heat half the oil in a small saucepan. Add tomatoes, salt, pepper to taste and sugar. Cook for 10 minutes or until sauce consistency, stirring frequently. Heat remaining oil in a large frying pan or saucepan. Add onion and garlic and cook until onion is clear. Stir in green pepper, courgettes and eggplant. Cover and cook slowly until vegetables are tender, stirring frequently. Add tomato mixture to the vegetables. Stir to combine. Serve hot.

SALMON AND PASTA NIÇOISE SALAD

SALAD
250 g small seashell pasta
200 g green beans
12 cherry tomatoes, halved
210 g can salmon, drained and roughly
    flaked
4 hard-boiled eggs, shelled and
    quartered
16–20 pitted black olives (preferably
    Kalamata olives)

DRESSING
¼ cup extra virgin olive oil
¼ cup lemon juice
2 tablespoons chopped parsley
1 tablespoon wholegrain mustard
freshly ground black pepper to season

Cook the pasta according to instructions on the packet. Tip into a sieve and refresh under cold running water. Drain thoroughly. Trim ends from beans. Plunge beans into boiling water. Allow to return to the boil, then cook for 1 minute or until just tender. Tip into a sieve and refresh under cold running water. Drain. Combine all salad ingredients in a bowl. To make the dressing, combine all ingredients. Mix well. Pour dressing over salad and toss lightly to combine.

SALMON AND PASTA NIÇOISE SALAD # 74

SMOKED CHICKEN, PAWPAW AND MACADAMIA NUT SALAD # 77
SPINACH, FETA AND BACON SALAD # 77

SPINACH SALAD ◈ 78

78 ◈ TANDOORI CHICKEN SALAD

WARM GINGER CHICKEN, CRISPY NOODLE
AND CASHEW NUT SALAD ◈ 81

82 ◈ WILD RICE SALAD

SMOKED CHICKEN, PAWPAW AND MACADAMIA NUT SALAD

DRESSING

½ pawpaw
1 tablespoon lemon or lime juice
1 tablespoon extra virgin olive oil
¼ cup loosely packed coriander leaves
freshly ground black pepper to season

SALAD

½ pawpaw
2 cups shredded smoked chicken
4 handfuls mixed salad greens,
    washed and dried
2 spring onions, sliced
½ cup salted macadamia nuts, roughly
    chopped

To make the dressing, cut pawpaw in half and remove seeds. Reserve half for the salad. Peel and roughly chop remaining half. Place in a food processor with remaining dressing ingredients. Blend until smooth. For the salad, cut pawpaw half into narrow slices, then peel. Cut slices into 3–4 cm lengths. Place chicken in a bowl. Pour half the dressing over the chicken and toss to coat. Place remaining dressing in a small jug to accompany the salad. To serve, place a handful of salad greens on each serving plate. Top with chicken, pawpaw, spring onions and nuts. Serve with fresh crusty bread, accompanied by jug of dressing.

SPINACH, FETA AND BACON SALAD

DRESSING

¼ cup extra virgin olive oil
2 tablespoons balsamic vinegar
1 tablespoon lemon juice
1 teaspoon brown sugar
salt and freshly ground black pepper
    to season

SALAD

3 slices toast-cut bread
2 tablespoons extra virgin olive oil
8 rashers rindless bacon, roughly
    chopped
150 g baby spinach leaves, washed
    and dried
200 g feta cheese, diced
¼ cup toasted pine nuts (optional)

To make the dressing, combine all ingredients. Mix well. For the salad, cut bread into small cubes. Heat oil in a frying pan. Toss bread over a medium heat until golden. Remove from pan. Add bacon and cook for 5–6 minutes until beginning to crisp. Remove from pan. Cool. Place all salad ingredients in a bowl. Pour over dressing and toss lightly to combine.

SPINACH SALAD

SERVES 4–6

1 bunch spinach
6–8 mushrooms, sliced
2 spring onions, sliced
1 orange, peeled and segmented
3 rashers bacon, cooked and diced
¼ cup French Dressing (see page 225)
2 hard-boiled eggs, chopped
¼ cup toasted flaked almonds

Tear spinach into bite-sized pieces and place in a salad bowl. Add mushrooms, spring onions, orange segments and bacon. Chill before serving. Add French Dressing and toss. Garnish with eggs and flaked almonds.

TANDOORI CHICKEN SALAD

SERVES 4 AS A LIGHT MEAL

4 single boneless skinless chicken
  breasts
¼ cup tandoori curry paste
2 tablespoons natural unsweetened
  yoghurt
4 handfuls mixed salad greens
1 tablespoon extra virgin olive oil
1 tablespoon wine vinegar
2 bananas
1 tablespoon lemon juice
¼ cup coconut, toasted (see page 230)
4 naan
1 avocado, sliced
mango chutney to serve

Place chicken between two sheets of plastic wrap. Pound with a heavy object (such as a rolling pin) to flatten to an even thickness of 1 cm. Place in a single layer in a plastic or glass dish. Combine curry paste and yoghurt and spread over chicken. Cover and refrigerate for 1 hour. Preheat oven grill. Grill chicken for 6–8 minutes on each side or until cooked through. Cool. Place salad greens in a bowl. Sprinkle over oil and vinegar and toss to coat. Peel and slice bananas. Place in a small bowl. Add lemon juice and toss to coat, then sprinkle over coconut, tossing to coat. To assemble salad, place a naan on individual serving plates. Top with salad greens. Slice chicken and arrange with avocado on top of salad greens. Place a spoonful of banana slices on the side and serve with a dollop of mango chutney.

THAI-STYLE BEEF SALAD

DRESSING

¼ cup soy sauce

¼ cup fish sauce

1 tablespoon canola oil

2 tablespoons lime or lemon juice

2 tablespoons chopped mint

2 tablespoons chopped coriander

2 cloves garlic, crushed

1 small red chilli, seeded and finely
  chopped

SALAD

750 g piece eye fillet steak

salt and freshly ground black pepper

canola oil

2 courgettes

2 carrots

150 g green beans, trimmed and halved

1 red capsicum, seeded and thinly
  sliced

1 yellow capsicum, seeded and thinly
  sliced

12–16 cherry tomatoes, halved (or 4
  regular tomatoes, quartered)

To make the dressing, combine all ingredients. Mix well. Preheat oven to 220°C. Season beef all over with a little salt and pepper. Heat oil in a heavy-based frying pan until pan is very hot. Cook beef for 3–4 minutes, turning regularly, until meat is seared all over. Transfer to a roasting dish. Bake for 10–12 minutes. The meat should be medium-rare. Set aside to cool. Meanwhile, prepare the vegetables. Trim ends off courgettes and carrots. Peel carrots. Using a vegetable peeler, peel long strips from the courgettes and carrots. Plunge into boiling water for 10 seconds to blanch. Tip into a sieve and refresh under cold running water. Blanch beans in the same way for 30 seconds. Tip into a sieve and refresh under cold running water. Slice beef thinly. Place all salad ingredients in a bowl. Pour over dressing and toss to combine.

TUNA PASTA SALAD

DRESSING
¾ cup mayonnaise
2 tablespoons lemon juice
1 tablespoon wine vinegar
1 teaspoon wholegrain mustard
2 tablespoons chopped parsley
salt and freshly ground black pepper
  to season

SALAD
500 g frilled shell pasta
2 red onions, diced
4 gherkins, diced
1 red capsicum, seeded and diced
2 carrots, peeled and cut into
  matchsticks
8 cherry tomatoes, halved (or 2 regular
  tomatoes, quartered)
185 g can tuna in brine, drained

To make the dressing, combine all ingredients. Mix well. For the salad, cook pasta according to the instructions on the packet. Drain in a sieve and cool under cold running water. Drain thoroughly. Combine all salad ingredients in a bowl. Pour dressing over and toss lightly to combine.

WARM GINGER CHICKEN, CRISPY NOODLE AND CASHEW NUT SALAD

4 single boneless skinless chicken
  breasts
¼ cup soy sauce
2 tablespoons lemon juice
1 tablespoon peanut oil
1 tablespoon finely grated root ginger
2 carrots, peeled
10 cm length telegraph cucumber
2 cups mung beans
2 cups crispy noodles
½ cup roasted salted cashew nuts

DRESSING
2 tablespoons soy sauce
1 tablespoon sesame oil
1 tablespoon lemon juice
1 tablespoon chopped coriander
coriander leaves to garnish

Place chicken between two sheets of plastic wrap. Pound with a heavy object (such as a rolling pin) to flatten to an even thickness of 1 cm. Place in a single layer in a plastic or glass dish. Combine first measures of soy sauce, lemon juice, peanut oil and ginger. Pour over chicken, turning to coat. Cover and refrigerate for at least 1 hour. Using a vegetable peeler, peel strips from the carrots. Plunge into boiling water for 30 seconds. Tip into a sieve and refresh under cold running water. Drain. Cut cucumber into diagonal slices, then cut slices in half lengthwise. Grill or barbecue chicken for 6–8 minutes on each side or until cooked through. Stand for 3–4 minutes before slicing. Combine chicken, carrot ribbons, cucumber, mung beans, noodles and nuts in a bowl. To make the dressing, combine all ingredients. Pour dressing over salad and toss to combine. Pile salad onto 4 serving plates. Garnish with coriander leaves and serve immediately.

WARM MEDITERRANEAN LAMB SALAD

1 small eggplant
2 courgettes
about ¼ cup extra virgin olive oil
1 red capsicum, roasted (see page 232
   for method)
1 yellow capsicum, roasted (see page
   232 for method)
250 g lamb fillets
salt and freshly ground black pepper
1 red onion, thinly sliced
5–6 canned artichoke hearts, halved
   (optional)

DRESSING

3 tablespoons extra virgin olive oil
1 teaspoon finely grated orange zest
2 tablespoons freshly squeezed
   orange juice
1 teaspoon liquid honey
2 tablespoons chopped basil
salt and freshly ground black pepper
   to season

Trim ends off eggplant and courgettes. Cut vegetables lengthwise into 5 mm thick strips. Preheat oven grill. Brush vegetables all over with olive oil. Place in a single layer on a baking tray. Grill for 4–5 minutes, turning occasionally, until vegetables are cooked through and golden. Cut capsicums into 1 cm wide strips. Season lamb fillets with salt and pepper. Heat a little oil in a heavy-based frying pan. Cook lamb for 8–10 minutes, turning occasionally. The lamb should be slightly pink on inside. Set aside for 4–5 minutes before slicing. To make the dressing, combine all ingredients in a bowl. Mix well. Combine all salad ingredients in a bowl. Pour over dressing. Toss lightly to combine. Serve salad immediately, accompanied by fresh bread.

WILD RICE SALAD

1½ cups wild rice
½ cup toasted pistachio nuts
3 spring onions, chopped
1 red capsicum, cored, seeded and
   diced
¼ cup chopped sundried tomatoes
100 g diced feta cheese, or 4 rashers
   rindless bacon, diced and cooked
   until crisp

DRESSING

2 tablespoons extra virgin olive oil
2 tablespoons freshly squeezed
   orange juice
2 tablespoons chopped fresh herbs
   (e.g. parsley or coriander)
1 teaspoon wholegrain mustard

Cook rice according to instructions on packet. Tip into a sieve and rinse under cold running water. Drain thoroughly. Combine all salad ingredients in a bowl. To make the dressing, combine all ingredients. Mix well. Pour dressing over salad and toss to combine.

FINGER FOOD

ANTIPASTO

Antipasto is an Italian term for 'before the meal' and can include any of the following types of finger foods: Hummus (see page 89), olives, sliced meats such as salami, prosciutto, smoked pork or beef, semi-dried tomatoes (see page 216), feta and olive preserve (see page 211), roasted capsicums (see page 232), canned artichoke hearts, cherry tomatoes. The following recipes from the Preserves section of this book can be included on an antipasto platter: Chargrilled Capsicums with Garlic and Rosemary (see page 211), Marinated Olives with Herbs (see page 215) and Oven-dried Tomatoes (see page 216). Accompany an antipasto platter with fresh crusty bread or crostini (see below).

BACON-WRAPPED BANANAS

MAKES 8

2 bananas
lemon juice
4 rashers bacon

Peel bananas and cut each into 4 pieces. Brush with lemon juice. Cut each rasher of bacon in half. Wrap bananas in bacon. Secure with toothpicks. Grill on both sides until bacon is cooked. Serve warm.

BLUE CHEESE SPREAD

250 g blue cheese
150 g cream cheese
1 small onion, chopped
2 tablespoons softened butter
1 tablespoon Worcestershire sauce
dash Tabasco sauce
2 tablespoons dry sherry
pumpernickel bread and Crostini (see right) to serve
tiny sprigs of fresh herbs to garnish

Crumble blue cheese into the bowl of a food processor. Add cream cheese, onion, butter, Worcestershire and Tabasco sauces and sherry. Process until smooth. Transfer to a bowl. Cover and refrigerate until firm. When ready to use, spread on pumpernickel bread or crostini. Garnish with sprigs of fresh herbs.

CROSTINI
Cut a French loaf into 4 mm thick slices. Brush both sides of bread with olive oil. Place in a single layer on a baking tray. Bake at 190°C for 10–12 minutes, until golden. Cool. Store in an airtight container until required. Stored thus, crostini will keep for up to 1 week.

CHEESE BALL

250 g cream cheese
1 cup grated tasty cheddar cheese
1 pickled onion, finely chopped
2 tablespoons finely chopped parsley
2 tablespoons finely chopped gherkin
1 tablespoon tomato sauce
1 teaspoon Worcestershire sauce
few drops Tabasco sauce
¼ teaspoon paprika
½ cup chopped walnuts, approximately
crackers or sliced fresh bread to serve

Combine cheeses in a bowl. Add pickled onion, parsley, gherkin, tomato, Worcestershire and Tabasco sauces and paprika. Beat well to combine. Shape into a ball. Roll in chopped walnuts until well coated. Wrap and chill until firm. Serve with crackers or sliced fresh bread.

CHICKEN LIVER PÂTÉ

MAKES ABOUT 2 CUPS

1 onion
1 clove garlic
50 g butter
350 g chicken livers
2 teaspoons prepared French mustard
2 tablespoons sherry
¼ teaspoon salt
1 tablespoon drained green
   peppercorns
coarsely ground black pepper
fresh herbs

Peel onion and chop roughly. Crush, peel and chop garlic. Melt butter in a frying pan and sauté onion and garlic for 5 minutes or until clear. Place in a blender or food processor. Remove any fat or gristle from chicken livers. Chop livers and add to onion pan. Sauté until they lose their pinkness. Add to onion in blender with mustard, sherry and salt. Blend until smooth. Mix in peppercorns and pack into a serving dish. Coarsely grind black pepper over and garnish with fresh herbs.

DEVILLED ALMONDS

MAKES 2 CUPS

2 tablespoons canola oil
2 cups blanched almonds
¼ teaspoon chilli powder
   (approximately)
2 teaspoons salt

Heat oil in a frying pan. Add almonds and stir continuously until golden. Drain almonds on paper towels. Combine chilli and salt. Toss almonds in this mixture to coat. Leave to dry.

DEVILS ON HORSEBACK

MAKES 8

8 well-soaked or cooked prunes
4 rashers bacon

Remove stone from prunes. Cut each rasher of bacon in half. Wrap each prune in bacon. Secure with a toothpick. Place on an oven tray. Grill on both sides until bacon is cooked. Serve warm.

FELAFEL WITH YOGHURT SAUCE

MAKES 36

YOGHURT SAUCE
1 cup natural unsweetened yoghurt
1 clove garlic, crushed
1 tablespoon chopped parsley
1 tablespoon tahini
¼ teaspoon ground cumin
freshly ground black pepper to season

FELAFEL
2 × 300 g cans chickpeas in brine
1 stalk celery, chopped
1 onion, chopped
1 teaspoon crushed garlic
2 tablespoons Edmonds standard
 grade flour
2 tablespoons tahini
1 teaspoon ground cumin
½ teaspoon turmeric
½ teaspoon salt
freshly ground black pepper to season
Edmonds standard grade flour to coat
canola oil to cook

To make the yoghurt sauce, combine all ingredients. Mix well. Cover and refrigerate until required. To make the felafel, place chickpeas, celery, onion, garlic, flour, tahini, cumin, turmeric, salt and pepper in a food processor. Blend to a coarse consistency. Transfer to a bowl. Cover and refrigerate for 1 hour. Spread a little flour onto a flat plate. Take large teaspoonfuls of mixture and roll into balls, then flatten slightly with the palm of the hand to make a little patty. Roll in flour to lightly coat. Pour oil into a frying pan to a level of 1 cm. Heat pan. Cook felafels for about 5 minutes, or until golden, turning once. Drain on paper towels. Serve with Yoghurt Sauce.

GUACAMOLE

MAKES ABOUT 1 CUP

1 ripe avocado
½ cup sour cream
2 teaspoons lemon juice
few drops Tabasco sauce
¼–½ teaspoon chilli powder
salt to season
sprig of fresh herbs to garnish
 (optional)

Remove flesh from avocado and mash. Mix in sour cream, lemon juice, Tabasco sauce and chilli powder. Season with salt to taste. Cover. Chill until ready to serve. Garnish with a sprig of fresh herbs.

BACON-WRAPPED BANANAS » 84

85 » CHICKEN LIVER PÂTÉ

DEVILS ON HORSEBACK » 86

86 » GUACAMOLE

HUMMUS (Chickpea dip)

MAKES ABOUT 1½ CUPS

1 cup chickpeas
1 onion, finely chopped
3 tablespoons tahini
1 teaspoon ground cumin
¼ cup canola oil
2 tablespoons lemon juice

Put the chickpeas into a bowl. Cover with boiling water. Stand for 1 hour. Drain. Cook in boiling, salted water for 1 hour or until tender. Drain and allow to cool. Put chickpeas into a food processor or blender. Add onion, tahini, cumin, oil and lemon juice. Process until smooth. Chill until ready to serve.

MINI MEATBALLS WITH DIPPING SAUCE

MAKES 40

450 g lean minced beef
1 red onion, finely diced
2 cloves garlic, crushed
½ cup finely chopped coriander leaves
1 teaspoon ground cumin
100 g pitted green olives, finely chopped
1 egg, beaten
salt and freshly ground black pepper
2 tablespoons canola oil

DIPPING SAUCE
¼ cup sweet chilli sauce
¼ cup tomato sauce
juice of 1 lime
1 tablespoon sesame oil
2 tablespoons soy sauce

Combine all the ingredients except the oil and shape into 40 small balls. Place in a roasting pan with the oil and bake in a preheated oven at 190°C for 15 minutes until well browned. To make the dipping sauce, combine all the ingredients in a glass jar. Shake well, and chill. Serve meatballs hot with the dipping sauce.

MIXED SATAYS WITH PEANUT DIP

MAKES 18

350 g piece fast-fry steak (e.g. rump, porterhouse, fillet)
350 g boneless skinless chicken (2 chicken breasts)
18 shelled raw king prawns
18 × 20 cm long wooden skewers
Quick Peanut Dip (see page 92)

MARINADE
¾ cup coconut milk
3 tablespoons soy sauce
3 tablespoons canola oil
3 cloves garlic, crushed
1 teaspoon ground cumin
1 teaspoon ground coriander

Remove any visible fat from the steak and chicken. Cut lengthwise into thin strips. Place beef, chicken and prawns in individual bowls. Make marinade by combining all ingredients. Divide marinade between the three bowls. Cover and refrigerate for 1–2 hours. Soak skewers in cold water for 30 minutes to prevent burning while cooking. Thread beef onto six skewers and chicken onto six skewers. Thread three prawns onto each of the remaining six skewers. Place beef and chicken skewers in a single layer on a baking tray. Preheat oven grill. Grill for 6–8 minutes, turning occasionally, then add prawn skewers and cook for a further 4–6 minutes until cooked through. Serve with Quick Peanut Dip.

PARMESAN AND GARLIC TWISTS

MAKES 8

DOUGH
1½ teaspoons sugar
300 ml warm water
1 tablespoon Edmonds active yeast
3 cups Edmonds high grade flour
1½ teaspoons salt
2 tablespoons pure olive oil

TOPPING
2 tablespoons pure olive oil
1 clove garlic, crushed
2–3 tablespoons freshly grated
    parmesan cheese
1 tablespoon finely chopped rosemary
rock salt to sprinkle (optional)

Dissolve the sugar in warm water. Sprinkle the yeast over the water and set aside in a warm place for 10 minutes until frothy. Combine the flour and salt in a large bowl. Stir in frothy yeast mixture and oil. Mix to a soft dough. Transfer the dough to a liberally floured surface and knead for 5 minutes until smooth and elastic. Divide the dough into eight equal portions. To make each twist, take a portion of the dough and divide in half. Roll each piece into a 20 cm long sausage shape. Twist the dough lengths together by using a dab of olive oil at the join and squeezing the dough ends to secure. Place the twists on a lightly greased oven tray, allowing room for spreading. To make the topping, combine oil and garlic. Brush the twists with the oil and garlic topping. Cover with plastic wrap and sit in a warm place for about 45 minutes until well risen. Sprinkle with parmesan cheese, rosemary and rock salt. Bake at 220°C for 10 minutes, then reduce temperature to 200°C and bake for a further 5 minutes until golden.

PROSCIUTTO-WRAPPED ASPARAGUS

MAKES 12 BUNDLES

36 slender asparagus spears
extra virgin olive oil to brush
6 slices prosciutto, halved lengthwise
Hollandaise Sauce (see page 226) to
    serve

Trim asparagus spears to an even length, removing the woody ends. Blanch asparagus in boiling water, or microwave until just tender. Drain in a sieve under cold running water to refresh. Drain thoroughly. Lay on a double thickness of paper towels, then pat dry with more paper towels. Brush spears lightly with a little olive oil. Bundle together three spears and wrap a strip of prosciutto around each bundle. Arrange on a serving plate. Serve accompanied by Hollandaise Sauce.

QUICK PEANUT DIP

1 teaspoon canola oil
1 small onion, finely chopped
1 cup crunchy peanut butter
¾ cup milk (or coconut milk)
1 tablespoon chilli sauce (optional)

Heat oil in a small saucepan. Cook onion for 4–5 minutes until soft. Add remaining ingredients to the pan. Stir over a low heat for 3–4 minutes until mixture is smooth and heated through. For a delicious snack, serve warm. Accompany with vegetable sticks or pita crisps.

SESAME CHICKEN STICKS

2 skinless boneless chicken breasts
1 tablespoon soy sauce
1 teaspoon canola oil
¾ cup sesame seeds
chilli sauce to serve

Cut chicken into 1.5 cm wide strips. Combine chicken, soy sauce and oil in a bowl. Mix well. Cover and refrigerate for at least 30 minutes. Place sesame seeds on a flat plate. Roll chicken sticks in the sesame seeds to cover. Transfer to a lightly oiled roasting dish. Bake at 220°C for 15 minutes until cooked through and golden, turning every 3–4 minutes. Serve hot, accompanied by a small bowl of chilli sauce.

NOTE: If desired, serve Sesame Chicken Sticks with Quick Peanut Dip (see above).

SESAME-MARINATED CHICKEN NIBBLES

¼ cup liquid honey
¼ cup hoisin sauce
3 tablespoons sesame seeds
2 tablespoons tomato sauce
2 tablespoons dry sherry
1 tablespoon sesame oil
1 tablespoon soy sauce
2 cloves garlic, crushed
750 g chicken nibbles

In a small bowl, combine all ingredients except chicken nibbles. Mix well. Place chicken nibbles in a medium bowl. Pour over marinade. Toss nibbles until evenly coated. Cover and refrigerate for at least 2 hours, or up to 8 hours. Place nibbles in a shallow roasting dish. Bake at 200°C for 20 minutes, turning occasionally, until golden and cooked through.

SESAME-MARINATED CHICKEN NIBBLES ⬥ 92

94 ⬥ SPICY CAJUN POTATO WEDGES

SPRING ROLLS WITH CHILLI DIPPING SAUCE ⬥ 94

95 ⬥ SUSHI

SPICY CAJUN POTATO WEDGES

3 tablespoons Edmonds standard
   grade flour
3 teaspoons Cajun spice mix
½ teaspoon chilli powder
6 medium potatoes, washed
canola oil to coat
sour cream to serve
paprika to garnish

Combine flour, Cajun spice mix and chilli powder. Place in a plastic bag. Cut potatoes in half lengthwise, then cut each half into four wedges. Place wedges in a bowl. Pour over just enough oil to lightly coat the potatoes once tossed thoroughly. Transfer wedges to the plastic bag. Twist top of bag and shake vigorously to coat. Preheat oven to 220°C, placing a large roasting dish in the oven to heat. Add wedges. Bake for 40 minutes, turning occasionally, until potatoes are cooked through and golden. Accompany with sour cream that has been lightly sprinkled with paprika.

SPRING ROLLS WITH CHILLI DIPPING SAUCE

CHILLI DIPPING SAUCE
¼ cup rice wine vinegar
1 tablespoon sweet chilli sauce
1 tablespoon brown sugar
1 teaspoon grated root ginger

SPRING ROLLS
100 g vermicelli noodles
1 tablespoon canola oil
300 g lean pork mince
2 cloves garlic, crushed
1 tablespoon finely grated root ginger
2 spring onions, finely chopped
3 tablespoons sweet chilli sauce
1 tablespoon fish sauce
2 tablespoons chopped coriander
1 tablespoon Edmonds Fielder's
   cornflour
2 tablespoons water
20 spring roll wrappers
canola oil to cook

To make the dipping sauce, combine all ingredients. Mix well. To make the spring rolls, place vermicelli in a bowl. Pour over warm water to cover. Stand for 10 minutes. Drain, then roughly chop. Heat oil in a frying pan. Cook pork, garlic and ginger for 2 minutes, stirring often, until pork is cooked. Add vermicelli, spring onions, chilli sauce, fish sauce and coriander. Cook for 1–2 minutes until combined. Set aside to cool. Mix cornflour to a paste with water. Take one spring roll wrapper at a time. Brush edges lightly with cornflour paste. Place a tablespoonful of mixture along one edge of the wrapper, leaving a 1.5 cm border for folding over filling. Fold edges in and roll up to enclose. Pour oil into a saucepan to a level of 5 cm. Heat. Cook spring rolls for 1–2 minutes, or until golden, removing with a slotted spoon as they are ready. Drain on paper towels. Place dipping sauce in a small dish in the middle of a platter. Pile spring rolls onto platter and serve immediately.

SUSHI

2 cups short-grain rice
3 cups cold water
⅓ cup sugar
⅓ cup rice vinegar
1 level tablespoon salt
7 toasted nori sheets
2 teaspoons wasabi paste

FILLING COMBINATIONS
(all finely sliced into strips)
— pickled ginger, telegraph cucumber
  and red capsicum
— smoked salmon, telegraph
  cucumber and yellow capsicum
— carrot, telegraph cucumber and red
  capsicum

DIPPING SAUCE
3 tablespoons light soy sauce
¼ teaspoon wasabi paste

Place rice in a sieve. Rinse thoroughly under cold running water. Place rice and water in a saucepan. Set aside for 30 minutes. Cover pan and bring to the boil over a high heat. Reduce heat to very low and simmer for about 15 minutes — until all the water has been absorbed. Turn off heat and stand for 15 minutes. Combine sugar, vinegar and salt. Gradually add to the rice, tossing rice with a fork. Cover and set aside for 10 minutes to cool slightly. Divide into seven equal portions. To assemble, place a sheet of nori, rough-side up, on a damp bamboo sushi mat. Spread one portion of rice over the nori. Using the wasabi paste sparingly, spread a narrow line across one end of the rice, 2.5 cm from the edge. Arrange filling ingredients of choice along the line of wasabi. Starting at the edge with the filling, use the bamboo mat to help roll the sushi into a tight log, pressing down firmly as you roll. Using a sharp knife, trim off ends, then cut log into five equal portions. To make the dipping sauce, combine soy sauce and wasabi paste. Transfer to a serving dish.

LIGHT MEALS
AND SOUPS

BROCCOLI AND BLUE CHEESE FILO PIE

1 small head broccoli, cut into florets
1 tablespoon water
3 tablespoons melted butter
6 sheets Edmonds filo pastry, thawed
100 g blue cheese, crumbled
5 eggs, lightly beaten
1½ cups milk
½ cup cream
salt and freshly ground black pepper
  to season
¼ cup finely grated parmesan cheese

Place broccoli in a microwave-proof dish. Add water. Cover and cook on high power for 45 seconds. Tip into a sieve and refresh under cold running water. Drain thoroughly. Brush a 25 × 20 cm baking dish with melted butter. Line with a sheet of filo, extending the pastry over the ends of the dish. Brush with melted butter. Repeat the last two steps, layering the sheets of pastry and brushing with butter. Scatter broccoli and cheese over base of dish. Whisk together eggs, milk, cream and salt and pepper. Pour into dish. Sprinkle over parmesan. Scrunch up the overhanging pastry and place on the edge of the pie. Bake at 190°C for 30–35 minutes or until egg mixture is set. Stand for 4–5 minutes before serving. Serve with a tossed salad.

CHICKEN ENCHILADAS

400 g can tomatoes in juice
113 g can jalapeño peppers
1 teaspoon ground coriander
½ teaspoon salt
250 g sour cream
2 tablespoons canola oil
2 cups chopped cooked chicken
1 small onion, finely chopped
salt and freshly ground black pepper
8 × 20 cm round flour tortillas
¾ cup grated tasty cheddar cheese

Put tomatoes in juice, jalapeño peppers, coriander and salt into a food processor or blender. Process until smooth. Add sour cream and process to combine. Set aside. Heat oil in a saucepan. Add chicken and onion. Cook for about 5 minutes, stirring constantly, until onion is soft. Season to taste with salt and pepper. Lay tortillas on a flat surface. Spread with tomato mixture. Divide chicken mixture between the tortillas, spreading in a log shape along one edge. Roll up like a sponge roll. Place seam side down in ovenproof dish. Repeat with remaining tortillas and chicken. Pour remaining tomato mixture over. Sprinkle with cheese. Cover dish with lid or foil. Cook at 180°C for 30 minutes. Remove lid, then grill until golden.

CRISPY-SKINNED POTATOES WITH BACON AND AVOCADO FILLING

SERVES 4

4 potatoes, washed
oil to brush
knob of butter
1 tablespoon pure olive oil
4 rashers rindless bacon, chopped
1 firm, ripe avocado
2 spring onions, chopped
¾ cup grated tasty cheddar cheese
salt and freshly ground black pepper

Lightly brush potatoes with oil. Bake at 180°C for 1–1½ hours until potatoes are tender when pierced with a sharp knife. Cut potatoes in half lengthwise. Scoop out flesh, leaving a 5 mm thick potato shell. Place potato flesh in a bowl. Brush inside of potato shells lightly with oil. Place on a baking tray. Bake at 250°C for 12–15 minutes until golden. Add butter to potato flesh and mash to a smooth consistency. Heat oil in a frying pan. Cook bacon until beginning to crisp. Cut avocado in half. Remove stone. Peel, then dice. Add bacon, avocado, spring onions and cheese to potato. Season to taste with salt and pepper. Pile filling back into the shells. Bake at 200°C for 20 minutes to heat through.

CURRIED VEGETABLE PARCELS

MAKES 6

2 tablespoons canola oil
2 cups small cauliflower florets
2 cups peeled, seeded and finely diced pumpkin
1 onion, chopped
1 courgette, thinly sliced
1 red capsicum, seeded and sliced
1 green capsicum, seeded and sliced
1 tablespoon curry powder
1 teaspoon crushed garlic
6 tablespoons coconut-milk powder
½ cup warm water
18 sheets Edmonds filo pastry
50 g butter, melted
relish or chutney to serve

Heat the oil in a heavy-based frying pan. Cook all the vegetables and the curry powder for 5 minutes over a low–medium heat, stirring frequently. Cover the pan and cook for about 10 minutes, stirring occasionally, until the vegetables are tender. Add the garlic. Mix the coconut-milk powder and water to a smooth paste. Add to the pan, stirring well. Simmer, uncovered, for 6–8 minutes or until the sauce is thick. Cool. For each parcel, lay a sheet of filo pastry on a flat surface. Brush with melted butter. Layer two more sheets of the pastry on top, brushing between each sheet with butter. Fold pastry in half widthways. Spoon one-sixth of the vegetable mixture in a line (about 8 cm long) along one long edge of the pastry. Roll up to form a log. Squeeze the pastry together around each end of the filling to form a cracker. Place the parcels on a greased baking tray. Brush with melted butter. Bake at 190°C for 12–15 minutes until golden. Serve immediately accompanied by relish or chutney.

BROCCOLI AND BLUE CHEESE FILO PIE ⬧ 97

98 ⬧ CURRIED VEGETABLE PARCELS

EASY SEAFOOD TORTILLA ⬧ 100

100 ⬧ FETA, OLIVE AND SUNDRIED TOMATO CALZONE

EASY SEAFOOD TORTILLA

16 cooked mussels, roughly chopped
1 cup cooked shrimps, chopped
2 spring onions, finely sliced
1 teaspoon grated root ginger
2 tablespoons sweet chilli sauce
salt and freshly ground black pepper
2 cups Edmonds standard grade flour
1 teaspoon Edmonds baking powder
1 cup soda water
2 tablespoons canola oil

In a large bowl, mix together the mussels, shrimps, spring onions, ginger and sweet chilli sauce. Season to taste with salt and black pepper. Sift the flour and baking powder and add to the seafood mix. Mix in the soda water until the mixture is just combined. Do not overmix. Heat the oil in a medium, non-stick frying pan. Spoon half the seafood mixture into the pan and spread it around the pan, making it into a full circle. Cook for about 6 minutes on one side, then carefully flip over using a spatula. Cook until golden brown on both sides. Remove from the pan, drain on kitchen paper and keep warm. Repeat with the second half of the mixture. Cut the tortillas into eighths. Serve immediately with salad and sweet chilli sauce.

FETA, OLIVE AND SUNDRIED TOMATO CALZONE

DOUGH
1½ teaspoons sugar
300 ml warm water
2 tablespoons Edmonds active yeast
3 cups Edmonds high grade flour
1½ teaspoons salt
¼ cup pure olive oil

FILLING
75 g olive tapenade
100 g feta cheese, cut into 1 cm dice
2 roasted capsicums (see page 232 for method), sliced
4 artichoke hearts, sliced
¼ cup chopped sundried tomatoes
½ cup grated mozzarella cheese

pure olive oil to brush
¼ cup freshly grated parmesan cheese

Dissolve the sugar in the warm water. Sprinkle the yeast over the water and set aside in a warm place for 10 minutes until frothy. Combine the flour and salt in a large bowl. Stir in the frothy yeast mixture and oil. Mix to a soft dough. Transfer the dough to a liberally floured surface and knead for 5 minutes until smooth and elastic. Place the dough in an oiled bowl. Turn the dough to coat with oil. Cover with plastic wrap and stand in a warm place for 45 minutes until the dough is well risen. Divide the dough into four equal portions. Roll each portion into a 20 cm round circle. Cover half of each circle with filling ingredients to within 1 cm of the edge of the dough — first, spread with the tapenade, then with layers of feta, capsicums, artichokes, sundried tomatoes and mozzarella. Lightly brush the edge of the dough with water. Fold the unfilled portion of dough over the filling and crimp edges together to seal. Transfer the calzone to a lightly greased baking tray. Brush lightly with oil. Sprinkle with parmesan. Bake at 220°C for 10 minutes, then reduce the temperature to 200°C and bake for a further 10–15 minutes until golden.

FRENCH ONION SOUP

3 tablespoons butter
6 medium onions, thinly sliced
1 teaspoon sugar
4 cups beef stock
salt
black pepper
¼ cup dry sherry
4–6 slices cheese on toast

Melt butter in a saucepan. Add onions and sugar. Cook slowly for 20 minutes or until onions are golden. Add beef stock. Bring to the boil then cover and simmer for 15 minutes. Season with salt and pepper to taste. Just before serving, add sherry. Grill cheese on toast. Cut into triangles or squares and place on soup.

HAM AND VEGETABLE FRITTATA

2 tablespoons pure olive oil
1 onion, finely chopped
1 cup small broccoli florets
2 cloves garlic, crushed
1 tablespoon Dijon mustard
8 eggs
salt and freshly ground black pepper
  to season
2 cups diced cooked potatoes (about 2
  large potatoes)
4 slices ham, diced
1½ cups grated tasty cheddar cheese

Heat oil in a heavy-based 25 cm frying pan with a heatproof handle. Cook onion, broccoli, garlic and mustard over a medium heat for 5 minutes. Lightly beat eggs and salt and pepper. Add potatoes and ham to pan, stirring to combine. Spread mixture evenly over base of pan. Reduce heat to low. Pour eggs evenly over vegetable mixture. Sprinkle with cheese. Cook for about 8 minutes until frittata is half cooked. Meanwhile, preheat oven grill. Place frittata under grill for 3–4 minutes until set and golden. Leave in pan for 5 minutes before cutting into wedges. Serve warm or cold.

KUMARA SOUP

25 g butter
1 large kumara, peeled and chopped
1 onion, chopped
1 large potato, chopped
1½ teaspoons hot curry powder
3 cups chicken stock
1 cup milk
salt and freshly ground black pepper
chives to garnish

Melt butter in a saucepan. Add kumara, onion, potato and curry powder. Cook for 5 minutes until onion is soft. Stir in stock and bring to the boil. Simmer gently until vegetables are tender. Purée in a food processor or blender until smooth. Stir in milk. Reheat until almost boiling. Season to taste with salt and pepper. Ladle into warm bowls. Garnish with chives.

LAMB SATAY

4 lean lamb leg steaks
1 tablespoon chopped coriander
2 teaspoons canola oil
1 teaspoon sambal oelek or chilli paste
bamboo skewers soaked in cold water
 for 30 minutes

SAUCE
¼ cup soy sauce
¼ cup chopped spring onions
1 teaspoon sambal oelek or chilli paste
2 tablespoons lemon or lime juice

Trim fat from meat, cut it into small cubes and put in a bowl. Add coriander, oil and sambal oelek. Leave to marinate for 30 minutes. Thread meat onto soaked bamboo skewers. Grill for 10 minutes or until just cooked, turning occasionally. Serve with sauce. To make the sauce, combine all ingredients.

LEEK AND POTATO SOUP

5 medium potatoes, peeled and
 chopped
2 teaspoons pure olive oil or butter
2 small leeks, thinly sliced
1 clove garlic, crushed
200 g bacon pieces, finely chopped
6 cups chicken stock
1 bay leaf
2 sprigs parsley
1 cup milk
¼ cup chopped parsley
salt and freshly ground black pepper

Cook potatoes in boiling water until tender. Drain and mash. Set aside. Heat oil in a large saucepan. Add leeks, garlic and bacon. Cook without colouring until leeks are tender. Pour in stock. Add bay leaf and parsley sprigs. Bring to the boil. Reduce heat and simmer for 20 minutes. Remove bay leaf and parsley sprigs. Add mashed potato. Simmer for 15 minutes. Stir in milk and chopped parsley. Season to taste with salt and pepper. Ladle into warm bowls. Garnish with a sprinkle of pepper.

MARINATED PORK SPARE RIBS

½ cup tomato sauce
½ cup soy sauce
½ cup plum sauce
1 tablespoon sweet chilli sauce (or
 more to taste)
1 teaspoon crushed garlic
1.5 kg pork spare ribs

Combine the four sauces and garlic. Mix well. Using a sharp knife, divide spare ribs into one or two bone sections. Place ribs in a single layer over the base of a roasting dish. Pour over marinade. Toss ribs until evenly coated. Cover with plastic wrap and refrigerate for at least 1 hour or up to 8 hours. Bake at 200°C for 12–15 minutes, turning regularly, until cooked through. Turn oven to grill and cook ribs for a further 5 minutes, turning two or three times, until lightly browned.

MEXICAN QUESADILLAS

2 cups shredded cooked chicken
1½ cups grated tasty cheddar cheese
½ cup bottled tomato salsa
4 gherkins, sliced (optional)
8 × 20 cm round flour tortillas

Combine chicken, cheese, salsa and gherkins in a bowl. Mix well. Lay four of the tortillas on a flat surface. Divide mixture between the tortillas, spreading to within 1 cm of the edge. Sandwich with remaining tortillas, pressing lightly to consolidate. Heat a large frying pan. Using a large fish slice, transfer one tortilla to the pan. Cook over a medium heat for 2 minutes. Carefully turn and cook for a further 2 minutes or until cheese has melted. Remove from pan. Repeat with remaining tortillas. To serve, cut into wedges.

MINI MEAT PIES

2 teaspoons canola oil
500 g lean beef mince
½ cup tomato sauce
2 tablespoons tomato paste
¾ cup water
salt and freshly ground black pepper
    to season
6 sheets Edmonds frozen flaky puff
    pastry, thawed
milk to seal and glaze

Heat oil in a frying pan. Cook mince for 4–5 minutes until browned. Stir in tomato sauce, tomato paste and water. Simmer over a low heat for 15 minutes, or until most of the liquid has been absorbed. Season to taste. Remove from heat. Cool. Using an 8 cm round biscuit cutter, stamp 20 rounds from pastry sheets. Press into deep-pan muffin tins. Spoon cold mixture into pastry cases. Brush edge of pastry lightly with milk. Using a 7 cm round biscuit cutter, stamp 20 tops from remaining pastry. Place over pies, pressing lightly around the edge to seal. Brush tops lightly with milk. Bake at 200°C for 16–18 minutes until golden. Cool in tins for 2–3 minutes before removing. Serve hot.

PUMPKIN AND FETA LASAGNE

150 g lasagne
1 cup firmly packed, grated, peeled
  pumpkin
250 g cottage cheese
100 g feta cheese, diced
1 spring onion, chopped
2 eggs
½ teaspoon ground nutmeg
salt and freshly ground black pepper
  to season
500 g bottled pasta sauce
1½ cups grated tasty cheddar cheese

Cook lasagne according to packet instructions. Tip into a sieve and cool under cold running water. Drain. Combine pumpkin, cottage cheese, feta, spring onion, eggs and nutmeg in a bowl. Mix well. Season to taste. Spread half of the pumpkin mixture over the base of a greased ovenproof dish. Cover with a single layer of lasagne. Spread over half the pasta sauce. Repeat the layers once more, ending with the pasta sauce. Sprinkle over cheese. Bake at 190°C for 20–25 minutes.

RUSTIC CARAMELISED ONION AND TOMATO TARTS

3 tablespoons pure olive oil
4 red onions, thinly sliced
2 tablespoons brown sugar
2 tablespoons balsamic vinegar
400 g Edmonds flaky puff pastry
24 cherry tomatoes, halved
salt and freshly ground black pepper
  to season
⅓ cup finely grated parmesan cheese
  to sprinkle

Heat oil in a heavy-based frying pan. Cook onions over a very low heat for 20 minutes, stirring regularly. Stir in brown sugar and vinegar and cook for a further 2 minutes. Cool. Roll pastry out into a 32 × 24 cm rectangle. Cut into four equal-sized rectangles. Line a baking tray with baking paper. Transfer pastry rectangles to the tray. Refrigerate for 15 minutes. Divide caramelised onion between the pastry, spreading evenly and leaving a 3 cm border. Arrange tomatoes cut-side up on top of onion. Season, and sprinkle with parmesan. Bake at 200°C for 20 minutes or until the pastry border is risen and golden. Accompany with a tossed salad.

SPICY BEAN NACHO PIE ◆ 108

108 ◆ SPICY LENTIL SOUP

SUMMER CALZONE ◆ 109

109 ◆ VEGETABLE, CASHEW NUT AND HOKKIEN NOODLE STIR-FRY

SPICY BEAN NACHO PIE

1 tablespoon pure olive oil
1 large onion, cut into wedges
1 large garlic clove, sliced
1 teaspoon ground coriander
2 tablespoons chopped coriander
1 teaspoon ground cumin
1 teaspoon crushed dried chillies
1 teaspoon sugar
400 g can whole peeled tomatoes
1 chicken or vegetable stock cube
2 × 300 g cans mixed beans, drained
60 g tortilla chips
¾ cup grated tasty cheddar cheese
salt and freshly ground black pepper
2 tablespoons sour cream

Heat oil in a frying pan. Fry onion for 5 minutes. Stir in garlic, ground and fresh coriander, cumin, chillies, sugar and tomatoes. Crumble in stock cube. Stir in beans and simmer for 10 minutes. Preheat grill to high. Transfer mixture to an ovenproof dish. Scatter with tortilla chips and cheese. Season to taste with salt and pepper. Grill until cheese melts. Serve with sour cream.

SPICY LENTIL SOUP

2 teaspoons butter
2 teaspoons canola oil
1 clove garlic, crushed
1 carrot, finely chopped
1 onion, finely chopped
1 stalk celery, finely chopped
1 teaspoon curry powder
1 cup brown lentils
250 g bacon bones
400 g can tomatoes in juice, chopped
4 cups beef stock
salt
black pepper
2 tablespoons chopped parsley

Heat butter and oil in a large saucepan. Add garlic, carrot, onion and celery. Cook until onion is clear. Stir in curry powder. Cook, stirring constantly, for 30 seconds. Add lentils, bacon bones, tomatoes and juice and stock. Cover. Bring to the boil, then reduce heat and simmer covered for 1½ hours or until lentils are cooked. Remove and discard bacon bones. Season with salt and pepper to taste. Serve garnished with parsley.

SUMMER CALZONE

DOUGH

1½ teaspoons sugar
300 ml warm water
2 tablespoons Edmonds active yeast
3 cups Edmonds high grade flour
1½ teaspoons salt
¼ cup pure olive oil

FILLING

2 tablespoons Pesto (see page 227)
1½ cups grated mozzarella cheese
2 large tomatoes, sliced
1 red capsicum, roasted (see page 232
    for method), sliced
40 g thinly sliced salami

freshly ground black pepper
pure olive oil to brush
rock salt or finely grated parmesan
    cheese to sprinkle

Dissolve sugar in the warm water. Sprinkle yeast over water and set aside in a warm place for 10 minutes until frothy. Combine flour and salt in a large bowl. Stir in frothy yeast mixture and oil. Mix to a soft dough. Transfer dough to a liberally floured surface and knead for 5 minutes until smooth and elastic. Place dough in an oiled bowl. Turn dough to coat with oil. Cover with plastic wrap and stand in a warm place for 45 minutes until dough is well risen. Divide dough in half. Roll each portion into a 25 cm round circle. Place one circle on a lightly greased baking tray. Spread with Pesto to within 1 cm of the dough edge. Sprinkle mozzarella cheese over the pesto, then top with tomato, red capsicum and salami. Season with pepper. Brush edge of dough with a little oil. Position the remaining circle of dough on top and seal edges with your fingertips. Brush top lightly with a little olive oil. Sprinkle with rock salt or parmesan cheese. Bake at 220°C for 10 minutes, then reduce temperature to 200°C and bake for a further 15–20 minutes until golden. Serve in wedges.

VEGETABLE, CASHEW NUT AND HOKKIEN NOODLE STIR-FRY

2 tablespoons canola oil
1 tablespoon finely grated root ginger
1 teaspoon crushed garlic
2 carrots, thinly sliced
1 small head broccoli, cut into small
    florets
100 g snow peas
2 heads shanghai choy, leaves
    separated
3 spring onions, sliced
½ cup roasted salted cashew nuts
¼ cup soy sauce
1 tablespoon sweet chilli sauce
400 g hokkien noodles

Heat oil in a wok or large heavy-based frying pan. Cook ginger and garlic for 2–3 minutes. Add carrots and broccoli and stir-fry for 3–4 minutes. Add snow peas, shanghai choy, spring onions and cashew nuts and stir-fry for 2 minutes. Add soy sauce and chilli sauce and stir through vegetables. Add noodles to pan and stir-fry for about 2 minutes until heated through. Serve immediately.

MAIN MEALS AND BARBECUES

BAKED PORK CHOPS WITH HONEY AND MUSTARD

SERVES 4

4 large bone-in pork chops
canola oil for brushing
2 cloves garlic, peeled and crushed
2 tablespoons Worcestershire sauce
2 tablespoons tomato purée
1 teaspoon chilli sauce
2 tablespoons lemon juice
3 tablespoons wholegrain mustard
¼ cup liquid honey

Rub or brush chops with oil. Heat a non-stick frying pan and fry chops on both sides until golden. Transfer to a shallow baking dish. Mix remaining ingredients. Stir mixture. Pour over chops. Bake at 200°C for 40 minutes, basting occasionally until sauce is thick and shiny. Serve chops coated with sauce, accompanied with mashed potatoes and green beans.

BEEF, CASHEW NUT AND VEGETABLE STIR-FRY IN BLACK BEAN SAUCE

SERVES 4

750 g lean, fast-fry steak
   (e.g. rump, fillet or porterhouse)
3 tablespoons soy sauce
2 tablespoons dry sherry
2 tablespoons sesame oil
1 onion, thinly sliced
2 carrots, peeled and thinly sliced
227 g can bamboo shoots, drained
¼ cup black bean sauce
½ cup water
2 teaspoons Edmonds Fielder's
   cornflour mixed to a paste with
   1 tablespoon water
1 cup mung bean sprouts
1 cup toasted cashew nuts
cooked rice or noodles to serve

Cut meat into 5 mm wide strips. Combine meat, soy sauce and sherry in a bowl. Stand for 20 minutes. Heat 1 tablespoon of the oil in a wok or heavy-based frying pan. Stir-fry onion and carrot for 4–5 minutes until soft. Remove from pan. Add remaining oil to pan. Stir-fry meat for 2–3 minutes over a high heat until just cooked through. Return onion and carrot to pan. Add bamboo shoots, black bean sauce and water. Stir well. Add cornflour paste and stir continuously until sauce thickens and comes to the boil. Add bean sprouts and nuts. Toss to combine. Serve immediately on a bed of cooked noodles or rice.

BEEF CASSEROLE

1 kg chuck or blade steak
2 tablespoons canola oil
1 large onion, chopped
¼ cup Edmonds standard grade flour
3 cups beef stock
2 carrots, sliced
salt and freshly ground black pepper
1 bay leaf
sprig of thyme
sprig of parsley
1 tablespoon Edmonds Fielder's
  cornflour
1 tablespoon water

Trim fat from meat and cut into 2.5 cm cubes. Heat oil in a heavy-based frying pan. Add onion and cook for 5 minutes until soft. Using a slotted spoon, remove onion and place in a casserole dish. Coat meat in flour. Add one quarter of meat and quickly brown on all sides. Remove from pan. Repeat with remaining meat, one quarter at a time. Place meat in dish with onions. Gradually add stock to saucepan, stirring. Bring to the boil. Add carrots. Season with salt and pepper. Make a bouquet garni with bay leaf, thyme and parsley. Add bouquet garni and liquid to casserole dish. Cover and bake at 160°C for 1¼ hours or until meat is tender. Remove bouquet garni. Mix cornflour to a paste with water. Stir into casserole then return to the oven for a further 15 minutes. Serve with mashed potatoes and seasonal vegetables of your choice.

BEEF AND MUSHROOM CASSEROLE
Replace half the beef stock with red wine. Add ¼ cup tomato purée and 1 cup sliced mushrooms.

BEEF AND MUSTARD CASSEROLE
At end of cooking time, stir in 1 tablespoon wholegrain mustard.

BEEF FAJITAS

500 g lean, fast-fry steak (e.g. rump,
  fillet or porterhouse)
2 teaspoons paprika
1 tablespoon ground cumin
½ teaspoon chilli powder
1 teaspoon dried oregano
¼ teaspoon salt
1 clove garlic, crushed
1 tablespoon lemon juice
2 tablespoons canola oil
1 large onion, sliced
1 red capsicum, seeded and thinly
  sliced
1 green or yellow capsicum, seeded
  and thinly sliced
flour tortillas, Guacamole (see page
  86) and sour cream to serve

Thinly slice meat and place in a bowl. Combine paprika, cumin, chilli powder, oregano, salt and garlic. Sprinkle over meat and toss to combine. Add lemon juice and toss. Heat 1 tablespoon of oil in a heavy-based frying pan. Cook onion and capsicums over a high heat for 5 minutes until soft. Remove from pan and keep warm. Add remaining oil to pan. Add meat and cook over a high heat for 6–8 minutes until browned. Return vegetables to pan and toss to heat through. Serve immediately with flour tortillas, Guacamole and sour cream.

NOTE: The quantities of paprika and chilli powder used in the above recipe produce a medium-spiced dish. For a milder flavour, use 1 teaspoon paprika and ¼ teaspoon chilli powder. For a spicier flavour, use 3 teaspoons paprika and 1 teaspoon chilli powder.

BAKED PORK CHOPS WITH HONEY AND MUSTARD ◈ 111

111 ◈ BEEF CASSEROLE

BEEF STROGANOFF ◈ 112

114 ◈ BEEF WELLINGTON

BEEF STROGANOFF

500 g rump steak
2 tablespoons butter
1 tablespoon canola oil
1 onion, sliced
150 g mushrooms, sliced
¼ cup white wine
¾ cup sour cream
1 tablespoon lemon juice
salt
pepper

Trim fat from meat. Cut meat into thin strips against the grain. Heat butter and oil in a frying pan. Add meat and quickly brown on both sides. Remove from pan and set aside. Add onion and mushrooms to pan. Cook until onion is clear. Return meat to pan. Add wine and sour cream. Reheat gently. Add lemon juice. Season with salt and pepper to taste. Serve with rice.

BEEF WELLINGTON

1.25 kg fillet of beef
freshly ground black pepper
2 tablespoons canola oil
250 g green peppercorn pâté
100 g button mushrooms, sliced
400 g Edmonds flaky puff pastry,
   thawed (or pre-rolled pastry)
1 egg yolk
1 tablespoon water

Trim fat from meat. Wrap string around fillet to maintain shape. Season all over with pepper. Heat oil in a heavy-based frying pan. To seal in juices, cook meat over a high heat until evenly browned. Transfer to a large roasting dish. Bake at 180°C for 10 minutes. Remove from oven and allow meat to cool completely. Remove string and discard. Beat pâté with a wooden spoon until smooth. Spread pâté over entire surface of meat. Press mushrooms into pâté on top of meat. Roll pastry into a rectangle about 25 × 35 cm. (The exact size required will depend on the size of the meat.) Place meat top-side down in centre of pastry. Trim pastry, allowing enough just to encase the meat with a small overlap. Whisk together egg yolk and water. Fold ends and edge of pastry over meat, brushing with egg mixture to seal. Place sealed-edge down in a baking dish. Brush all over with egg mixture. Decorate with pastry offcuts and brush these with egg mixture. Bake at 220°C for 5 minutes. Reduce heat to 180°C and cook for a further 35 minutes for medium-rare or 40 minutes for medium. Stand meat for 10 minutes before slicing. If desired, serve with gravy, or Green Peppercorn Sauce (see page 226).

BOEUF BOURGUIGNON ≫ 116

116 ≪ BOLOGNESE

BRAISED LAMB KNUCKLES IN A RICH GRAVY ≫ 117

117 ≪ CARBONARA

BOEUF BOURGUIGNON

750 g chuck steak
2 tablespoons Edmonds standard
    grade flour
salt
pepper
2 tablespoons canola oil
8 pickling onions
2 rashers bacon
2 cloves garlic, crushed
¾ cup red wine
½ cup beef stock
4 carrots, quartered lengthwise
sprig of parsley
sprig of thyme
bay leaf

Trim fat from meat. Cut meat into serving-sized pieces. Combine flour, salt and pepper. Coat meat in seasoned flour. Heat oil in a flameproof casserole dish. Add onions and bacon and cook until golden. Using a slotted spoon, remove from pan and set aside. Add half the meat and quickly brown on all sides. Repeat with remaining meat. Return onions and bacon to pan with garlic. Add wine and stock, stirring well. Add carrots. Make a bouquet garni from parsley, thyme and bay leaf. Add to casserole. Cover and bake at 180°C for 1½–2 hours or until meat is tender. Serve with French bread and salad.

BOLOGNESE

2 tablespoons pure olive oil
2 large onions, finely chopped
500 g mince
¼ cup tomato paste
400 g can tomatoes in juice
1 teaspoon basil
1 teaspoon oregano
4 cups water
salt
black pepper
500 g spaghetti, cooked
freshly grated parmesan cheese

Heat oil in a large frying pan. Add onion and cook until golden, stirring constantly. Stir in meat and quickly cook until browned on all sides. Add tomato paste. Push tomatoes and juice through sieve. Add to pan. Stir in basil, oregano and water. Bring to the boil, reduce heat and cook uncovered for 45 minutes or until mixture is a thick sauce consistency. Season with salt and pepper to taste. Serve over hot pasta garnished with parmesan cheese.

BRAISED LAMB KNUCKLES IN A RICH GRAVY

½ cup Edmonds standard grade flour
salt and freshly ground black pepper
8 lamb knuckles
2 tablespoons canola oil
1 onion, finely chopped
1 teaspoon crushed garlic
1½ cups red wine
¼ cup tomato purée
2 cups beef stock
1 tablespoon Edmonds Fielder's
   cornflour
1 tablespoon water
salt and freshly ground black pepper
3 sprigs rosemary
sprigs of rosemary to garnish

Season flour with salt and pepper. Place in a shallow dish. Trim excess fat from knuckles. Roll in the flour mixture to coat. Heat oil in a large, heavy-based frying pan. Cook four knuckles at a time, turning occasionally, until browned. Transfer to a roasting pan. Repeat with remaining knuckles. Cover roasting dish and bake at 150°C for 1 hour. Remove dish from oven and pour off excess fat. While knuckles are cooking, add onion to the frying pan and cook for 5 minutes until soft. Add garlic, wine, tomato purée and stock. Mix cornflour to a paste with water. Add to pan, stirring constantly until sauce thickens slightly and comes to the boil. Season. Pour over knuckles. Lay 3 sprigs rosemary on top. Cover dish tightly with foil. Bake at 150°C for 2 hours, turning knuckles occasionally. Serve with mashed potato or a combination of mashed potato and mashed kumara. Garnish with sprigs of rosemary.

CARBONARA

2 tablespoons pure olive oil
2 ham steaks, chopped
1 onion, chopped
200 g mushrooms, sliced
250 g sour cream
1 egg yolk
pepper
375 g pasta, cooked (e.g. seashells,
   fettucine)
1 tablespoon chopped parsley

Heat oil in a frying pan or saucepan. Add ham and onion. Cook until onion is clear and ham slightly browned. Stir in mushrooms and cook for a further 2 minutes. Remove from heat. In a bowl, beat sour cream and egg yolk together. Add this to ham mixture. Return to a low heat and cook, stirring constantly until sauce thickens slightly. Do not allow to boil. Season with pepper to taste. Add hot pasta. Stir to combine. Garnish with parsley.

CHARGRILLED VEGETABLE LASAGNE ⬥ 119

119 ⬥ CHEESY SESAME-COATED CHICKEN

CHICKEN CANNELLONI ⬥ 121

124 ⬥ CHICKEN PAPRIKA

CHARGRILLED VEGETABLE LASAGNE

TOMATO SAUCE

1 tablespoon pure olive oil
1 onion, finely chopped
2 × 400 g cans tomatoes in juice
1 teaspoon crushed garlic
salt and freshly ground black pepper
   to season
1 medium eggplant
4 courgettes
2 capsicums (any colour)
about ⅓ cup pure olive oil to brush

150 g wide lasagne
1½ cups grated tasty cheddar cheese

To make the tomato sauce, heat oil in a frying pan. Cook onion for 5 minutes until soft. Add tomatoes, garlic and seasonings. Break up tomatoes with a wooden spoon. Simmer for about 25 minutes until sauce is thick. While the sauce is cooking, prepare vegetables. Trim ends off eggplant and courgettes. Cut eggplant into 5 mm thick round slices and courgettes lengthwise into 5 mm thick slices. Halve capsicums. Core and seed, then cut into 2.5 cm wide strips. Brush vegetables all over with olive oil. Place eggplant slices in a single layer in a baking dish. Place under a preheated grill, turning regularly until vegetables begin to brown. Repeat this cooking process with the courgettes and capsicums. Cook lasagne in boiling water for about 10 minutes, until al dente. Drain. Lay half the lasagne over the base of a 20 × 24 cm rectangular ovenproof dish. Top with half the grilled vegetables, then half the tomato sauce. Repeat these layers, finishing with the sauce. Sprinkle with cheese. Bake at 180°C for 25–30 minutes. Stand for 5 minutes. Serve with a tossed salad and crusty bread.

CHEESY SESAME-COATED CHICKEN

8 chicken drumsticks
2 tablespoons Edmonds standard
   grade flour
2 tablespoons grated parmesan
   cheese
1 teaspoon chicken stock powder
¼ teaspoon mixed herbs
2 tablespoons dry breadcrumbs
2 teaspoons sesame seeds
canola oil

Remove skin from chicken. Moisten chicken slightly with water. Combine flour, parmesan cheese, stock powder, herbs, breadcrumbs and sesame seeds. Put this mixture into a plastic bag. Add two drumsticks to bag and shake to coat. Repeat with remaining chicken, coating only two at a time. Place drumsticks in a lightly oiled baking dish. Allow to stand for 15 minutes. Bake at 200°C for 25 minutes, or until juices run clear when tested. Turn chicken once or twice during the cooking time. Serve hot or cold.

CHICKEN AND AVOCADO RISOTTO

1.5 litres chicken stock, approximately
¼ cup pure olive oil
1 onion, finely sliced
2 cloves garlic, crushed
500 g Arborio rice
1 cup dry white wine
2 cups cooked diced chicken
½ cup freshly grated parmesan cheese
1 firm ripe avocado, peeled and diced
salt and freshly ground black pepper
   to season
2 tablespoons shredded basil leaves

Bring chicken stock to the boil in a saucepan. Heat oil in a heavy-based, deep-sided frying pan. Cook onion for 5 minutes until soft. Add garlic and rice and stir over a low heat for 2–3 minutes to toast the rice. Add wine and cook for 1 minute. Ladle over sufficient boiling stock to just cover the rice. Cook, stirring frequently and adding more stock to cover the rice as the liquid is absorbed. This will take about 18 minutes. Remove pan from the heat. Add chicken and parmesan to the pan. Stir to combine. Cover pan and stand for 3–4 minutes. Gently toss through avocado. Season. Pile onto warm serving plates. Garnish with shredded basil.

CHICKEN CANNELLONI

1 tablespoon pure olive oil
1 onion, chopped
1 teaspoon crushed garlic
2 × 400 g cans tomatoes in juice
¼ cup tomato paste
salt and freshly ground black pepper
   to season
2 cups cooked finely diced chicken
½ cup cottage cheese
12 instant cannelloni tubes
1½ cups grated tasty cheddar cheese

Heat oil in a frying pan. Cook onion for 5 minutes until soft. Add garlic, tomatoes and tomato paste, breaking up tomatoes with a wooden spoon. Simmer for 25–30 minutes until sauce is thick. Season to taste with salt and pepper. Place chicken and cottage cheese in a bowl. Add 1 cup of the tomato sauce. Mix well. Fill cannelloni tubes with chicken mixture. Place in a single layer in a greased baking dish. Spread remaining tomato sauce evenly over the pasta. Sprinkle with cheese. Bake at 180°C for 25–30 minutes. Serve with a tossed salad.

CHICKEN CHOW MEIN

2 boneless skinless chicken breasts
2 tablespoons soy sauce
2 teaspoons dry sherry
2 teaspoons Edmonds Fielder's
  cornflour
½ teaspoon grated root ginger
2 tablespoons canola oil
1 onion, quartered
2 cloves garlic, crushed
1 cup broccoli florets
½ cup sliced celery
1 red capsicum, seeded and sliced
½ cup chicken stock
2 teaspoons Edmonds Fielder's
  cornflour
¼ teaspoon freshly ground black
  pepper
1 tablespoon soy sauce
crispy noodles to serve

Cut chicken into strips. Combine chicken, first measure of soy sauce, sherry, first measure of cornflour and root ginger. Set aside to marinate for 30 minutes. Heat oil in a wok or large heavy-based frying pan. Add onion and garlic and cook for 5 minutes until onion is clear. Add chicken and quickly stir-fry until meat is browned all over. Add broccoli, celery and capsicum. Stir-fry until vegetables are bright in colour. In a bowl, combine stock, second measure of cornflour and pepper. Add to wok, stirring until mixture thickens and comes to the boil. Sprinkle with second measure of soy sauce. Toss. Serve with crispy noodles.

CHICKEN CURRY

2 tablespoons canola oil
1 onion, chopped
2 cloves garlic, crushed
2 teaspoons grated root ginger
2 medium potatoes, peeled and diced
2 stalks celery, sliced
4 boneless skinless chicken breasts,
  diced
2 tablespoons curry powder
2 tablespoons Edmonds standard
  grade flour
1½ cups chicken stock
½ cup cream

Heat oil in a large saucepan. Add onion, garlic, ginger, potato and celery. Cook for 5 minutes, stirring frequently. Add chicken and cook for 3–4 minutes, stirring constantly. Stir in curry powder and flour and cook for 30 seconds. Add stock. Cover pan and bring to the boil. Reduce heat and simmer for 25 minutes, stirring occasionally, until chicken is tender. Stir in cream. Serve with cooked rice.

CRISPY CHINESE BATTER

Edmonds Fielder's cornflour
1 egg white

Coat the items to be cooked with cornflour. Lightly beat egg white with a fork. Dip the coated items in egg white then deep-fry. Drain on absorbent paper.

CHICKEN PAPRIKA

4 chicken breasts, boned
2 tablespoons canola oil
1 large onion, chopped
2 teaspoons paprika
1 tablespoon Edmonds standard grade
  flour
1 cup chicken stock
250 g sour cream or 300 ml cream
1 tablespoon lemon juice
salt
black pepper

Remove skin and fat from chicken. Heat oil in a large frying pan. Add chicken and quickly brown on all sides. Remove from pan and set aside. Add onion and cook until clear. Stir in paprika and cook for 30 seconds. Stir in flour and cook, stirring, for 1 minute. Gradually add stock, stirring constantly. Bring to the boil. Return chicken to pan. Cover, reduce heat and simmer gently for 15 minutes. Stir in sour cream. Continue cooking gently for a further 10 minutes or until juices run clear when tested. Add lemon juice. Season with salt and pepper to taste. Serve with cooked rice.

CHICKEN STIR-FRY WITH CASHEWS

2 single boneless chicken breasts
1 tablespoon Edmonds Fielder's
  cornflour
1 egg white
2 tablespoons canola oil
2 stalks celery, sliced
6 spring onions, sliced
100 g button mushrooms, quartered
2 teaspoons grated root ginger
½ cup chicken stock
½ teaspoon sugar
2 teaspoons Edmonds Fielder's
  cornflour
1 tablespoon dry sherry
¼ cup roasted cashew nuts

Remove skin and fat from chicken. Cut meat in 2.5 cm cubes. Coat in first measure of cornflour then in lightly beaten egg white. Heat oil in a wok or large frying pan. Add chicken and cook until crisp and golden. Remove chicken from pan with a slotted spoon. Set aside. Add celery to pan and stir-fry until just tender. Add spring onions, mushrooms and ginger. Stir-fry until spring onions are bright green in colour. Blend stock, sugar, second measure of cornflour and sherry together. Add to pan. Cook, stirring until mixture boils and thickens slightly. Add chicken and cashews. Stir to heat through.

CHILLI AND CORIANDER MARINATED STEAK

4 pieces eye fillet, scotch fillet or rump
  steak
¼ cup sweet chilli sauce
2 tablespoons soy sauce
2 tablespoons chopped fresh
  coriander

Trim fat from steak if necessary. Mix chilli sauce, soy sauce and coriander together in a shallow dish. Place steak in marinade and turn to coat. Leave for 2 hours at room temperature or refrigerate overnight. Grill or barbecue to preferred doneness.

CHILLI CON CARNE

1 tablespoon canola oil
2 onions, chopped
1 clove garlic, crushed
1 green capsicum, chopped
500 g lean beef mince
1½ teaspoons chilli powder
1 cup water
290 g can tomato paste
¼ teaspoon oregano
425 g can red kidney beans, drained
cooked rice to serve
chives for garnish

Heat oil in a large frying pan. Add onions, garlic and capsicum. Cook for 5 minutes until onion and capsicum are soft. Stir in meat and cook until meat is browned. Add chilli powder, water, tomato paste and oregano. Bring to the boil, stirring constantly. Reduce heat and simmer gently for 30 minutes or until mixture is thick. Add kidney beans to pan. Cook for a further 3–4 minutes, stirring frequently. Serve on a bed of rice or with rice moulds. To make rice moulds, press cooked rice firmly into oiled teacups. Invert cup onto serving plate and tap gently to release the moulded rice. Garnish with snipped chives.

CRUNCHY-TOPPED FISH PIE

1 kg potatoes, cut into chunks
900 g white fish fillets (e.g. tarakihi, snapper or cod)
2 cups milk
1 bay leaf
50 g butter, plus extra
1 onion, chopped
50 g Edmonds standard grade flour
1 cup cream
175 g large shrimps
25 g fresh dill, finely chopped
1½ cups grated tasty cheddar cheese

Parboil potatoes for 8–10 minutes or until just tender. Drain well and set aside. Meanwhile, put fish pieces into a wide saucepan, pour over milk and add bay leaf. Bring to the boil, then simmer for 3 minutes. Cover and remove from heat. Leave to stand for 5 minutes or until fish is just cooked. Remove fish using a slotted spoon. Strain and reserve cooking liquid for the sauce. Lightly grease a 2 litre ovenproof dish. Flake fish into large chunks, removing any skin and bones, and put in the dish. Melt butter in a pan, add onion and fry for 3 minutes or until softened but not browned. Stir in the flour and cook for 1 minute. Remove pan from heat and slowly stir in reserved cooking liquid and cream. Return to the heat and cook, stirring until thickened, smooth and just boiling. Remove from heat and stir in shrimps and dill. Season with salt and pepper. Pour over fish. Toss a knob of butter with potatoes and 1 cup of the cheese. Season. Be careful not to break up potatoes. Scatter potatoes over sauce so it is well covered. Sprinkle over remaining cheese. Bake in oven at 200°C for about 30 minutes or until potatoes are golden.

FISH PIE

25 g butter
1 tablespoon milk
3 cups cooked mashed potatoes
¾ teaspoon salt
black pepper
1 tablespoon butter
1 tablespoon Edmonds standard grade
  flour
1 cup milk
500 g smoked fish, flaked, or 425 g can
  tuna, drained and flaked
1 tablespoon chopped parsley
2 hard-boiled eggs, chopped

Mix first measure of butter and milk into the potatoes, beating with a fork to combine. Season with salt and pepper to taste. Line a 20 cm pie dish with half the potatoes. Set remaining potatoes aside. Heat second measure of butter in a saucepan. Stir in flour and cook until frothy. Gradually add second measure of milk, stirring constantly until sauce boils and thickens. Remove from heat. Add fish, parsley and eggs. Pour this mixture into the lined pie dish. Cover with remaining potato. Bake at 190°C for 20 minutes or until pale golden.

FRESH TOMATO AND BASIL SAUCE

500 g ripe tomatoes
1 onion
1 clove garlic
1 tablespoon pure olive oil
1 teaspoon prepared minced chilli
½ cup chopped fresh basil
250 g farfalle pasta, cooked
freshly grated parmesan cheese

Blanch tomatoes in boiling water for 1 minute. Drain and plunge into cold water. Peel and remove stem end. Cut tomatoes roughly. Peel onion and chop finely. Crush, peel and chop garlic. Heat oil in a saucepan and sauté onion and garlic for 5 minutes or until onion is clear. Add chilli and sauté for 30 seconds. Add tomatoes and half the basil and cook sauce over a low heat for 15 minutes or until pulpy. Mix in remaining basil. Toss tomato and basil sauce through pasta. Garnish with grated cheese.

GINGER BEEF STIR-FRY

500 g skirt steak
1 tablespoon canola oil
1 tablespoon soy sauce
2 teaspoons grated root ginger
2 tablespoons canola oil
1 red pepper, cubed
1 green pepper, cubed
4 spring onions, sliced
2 teaspoons soy sauce
2 tablespoons white vinegar
2 teaspoons Edmonds Fielder's cornflour
½ teaspoon sugar
¼ cup beef stock

Trim fat from meat. Cut into thin strips against the grain. Put meat, first measure of oil, first measure of soy sauce and ginger in a bowl. Leave to marinate for 30 minutes. Heat half the second measure of oil in a wok. Add meat and quickly stir-fry until browned. Remove from wok. Repeat with remaining oil and meat. Return meat to wok. Add peppers and spring onions. Stir-fry until vegetables are bright in colour. In a bowl, mix second measure of soy sauce, vinegar, cornflour, sugar and stock to a smooth paste. Add to wok and cook for 1 minute or until liquid boils and thickens.

GINGER BEEF STIR-FRY » 127

129 » GRILLED FISH WITH PARMESAN CRUST

HAMBURGERS » 129

131 » INDIAN BEEF CURRY

GRILLED FISH WITH PARMESAN CRUST

½ cup fresh breadcrumbs (white or
   brown)
½ cup freshly grated parmesan cheese
1 tablespoon wholegrain mustard
2 tablespoons melted butter
1 teaspoon finely grated lemon zest
salt and freshly ground black pepper
   to season
4 fillets boneless white fish (e.g.
   gurnard, tarakihi, snapper)
lemon wedges to garnish

To make the crumb topping, combine
breadcrumbs, cheese, mustard, melted butter,
lemon zest and salt and pepper. Mix well. Preheat
grill. Pat fish fillets dry with paper towels. Place
on a greased baking tray. Divide crumb mixture
between fish fillets, spreading evenly to cover.
Grill for about 8–10 minutes (cooking time will
depend on the thickness of the fish). The fish is
cooked when the flesh turns white. Garnish with
lemon wedges. Serve with a tossed salad and
fresh bread.

HAMBURGERS

500 g lean beef mince
1 onion, finely chopped
1 clove garlic, crushed
2 tablespoons tomato sauce
2 tablespoons chopped herbs (e.g.
   parsley, oregano)
⅓ cup rolled oats
1 egg
salt and freshly ground black pepper
   to season
oil
4 hamburger buns
salad ingredients of your choice (e.g.
   lettuce leaves, sliced cheese, sliced
   tomato, sliced avocado, sliced
   cucumber)

To make the hamburger patties, combine mince,
onion, garlic, tomato sauce, herbs, rolled oats,
egg, salt and pepper in a bowl. Mix well. Divide
mixture into four equal portions. Shape into
patties about 9 cm in diameter. Place patties in
a single layer on a plate and cover with plastic
wrap. Refrigerate for 30 minutes. Pour sufficient
oil into a heavy-based frying pan to just cover
the base. Cook patties over a medium heat for
about 7 minutes on each side, until golden and
cooked through. While the patties are cooking,
prepare hamburger buns. Cut buns in half
horizontally. Place cut-side up on a baking tray.
Place under a preheated grill to toast lightly.
Layer salad ingredients of your choice and a
patty on the bottom half of each bun. Top with
other half of bun. Serve immediately.

INDIAN BEEF CURRY

500 g beef topside
1 onion
2 cloves garlic
2 tablespoons peanut oil
2 tablespoons finely chopped fresh
  ginger
2 teaspoons ground cumin
2 teaspoons garam masala
2 teaspoons ground coriander
½ teaspoon ground cloves
2 cups beef stock
1 cup natural unsweetened yoghurt
8 papadums

Trim fat from meat and cut meat into 2 cm cubes. Peel onion and chop finely. Crush, peel and chop garlic. Heat oil in a large saucepan and sauté onion and garlic for 5 minutes or until clear. Add ginger, cumin, garam masala, coriander and cloves. Sauté for 1 minute or until spices smell fragrant. Add meat and stock. Cover and simmer for 1–1½ hours or until meat is tender and stock reduced to about ½ cup. Stir in yoghurt. Bring to the boil and then reduce heat. Cook papadums, two at a time, in the microwave on high power for 1 minute or until papadums are crisp. Alternatively, cook papadums to packet directions in hot oil. Serve curry with cooked papadums and steamed rice.

ITALIAN BAKED FISH

1 onion
4 medium fish fillets, skinned and
  boned
400 g can tomatoes in juice
½ cup tomato purée
1 tablespoon prepared minced chilli
1 teaspoon dried basil
2 tablespoons capers
¼ cup pitted black olives
freshly ground black pepper

Peel onion and cut into rings. Place fish in an ovenproof dish. Arrange onion rings over fish. Roughly chop tomatoes. Mix tomatoes and juice, tomato purée, chilli, basil, capers and olives together. Pour over fish. Cover and bake at 180°C for 20–25 minutes or until fish is cooked. Season with freshly ground black pepper and serve hot.

LAMB AND PRUNE TAGINE

1 cup pitted prunes
1 cup boiling water
2 tablespoons Edmonds standard
   grade flour
1 teaspoon ground cumin
1 teaspoon ground coriander
1 teaspoon cinnamon
salt and freshly ground black pepper
   to season
750 g lean diced lamb
1 tablespoon canola oil
2 onions, finely chopped
2 teaspoons Edmonds Fielder's
   cornflour
1 tablespoon water
¼ cup sliced almonds to garnish
coriander leaves to garnish

Place prunes in a bowl. Pour over water and allow to soak for 30 minutes. Combine flour, spices, salt and pepper in a bowl. Add lamb and toss until evenly coated. Transfer to a casserole dish. Heat oil in a frying pan. Cook onion for 5 minutes until soft. Transfer to the casserole dish. Add prunes and water and stir well. Cover dish and bake at 180°C for 1–1½ hours until tender, adding a little more water if all the liquid is absorbed. Mix cornflour to a smooth paste with the water. Stir into meat, then cover and cook for a further 15 minutes. Garnish with almonds and coriander leaves. Serve with mashed potatoes and seasonal vegetables.

LAMB AND VEGETABLE STIR-FRY

500 g lean lamb leg steaks
2 tablespoons soy sauce
2 tablespoons dry sherry
1 tablespoon finely grated root ginger
3 tablespoons canola oil
1 onion, sliced
2 cloves garlic, crushed
3 stalks celery, sliced
1 carrot, peeled and thinly sliced
1 head broccoli, cut into small florets
¼ cup water
2 tablespoons soy sauce
2 tablespoons malt vinegar
425 g can baby corn, drained
2 teaspoons Edmonds Fielder's
   cornflour
1 tablespoon water
cooked rice to serve

Remove any visible fat from the meat. Cut lamb into 1 cm wide strips. Place in a bowl. Combine first measure of soy sauce, sherry and ginger. Pour over meat and stir. Set aside for 30 minutes. Heat 1 tablespoon of the oil in a wok or heavy-based frying pan. Stir-fry lamb over a high heat for 3–4 minutes until cooked through. Remove from pan. Heat remaining oil. Stir-fry onion, garlic, celery, carrot and broccoli for 4–5 minutes. Add first measure of water, soy sauce and vinegar. Cook for a further 3–4 minutes, stirring occasionally. Add corn and lamb. Cook for 2–3 minutes. Mix cornflour to a smooth paste with water. Add to wok, stirring until sauce thickens. Serve on a bed of rice.

LAMB CURRY

1½ tablespoons Edmonds standard
    grade flour
salt and freshly ground black pepper
750 g lean diced lamb
2 tablespoons canola oil
1 large onion, chopped
2 cloves garlic, crushed
1 tablespoon tomato paste
1½ teaspoons grated root ginger
1 teaspoon chopped fresh seeded chilli
1½ teaspoons ground cumin
1 teaspoon ground coriander
1 teaspoon ground cardamom
½ cup chicken stock
strips of red capsicum to garnish
poppadoms to serve

Combine flour, salt and pepper in a bowl. Coat meat in seasoned flour. Set aside. Heat oil in a large saucepan. Add onion and garlic and cook for 5 minutes until onion is clear. Remove with slotted spoon. Add half of the meat to pan and quickly brown all over. Remove from pan and repeat with remaining meat. Return meat and onion mixture to saucepan. Add tomato paste, ginger, chilli, cumin, coriander, cardamom and stock. Stir well. Bring to the boil. Cover, reduce heat and simmer gently for 1 hour or until meat is tender. Transfer to a warm serving dish. Garnish with strips of red capsicum. Serve with Cucumber and Mint Raita (see page 226) and poppadoms.

LASAGNE

MEAT SAUCE

2 tablespoons pure olive oil
1 onion, chopped
3 cloves garlic, crushed
500 g mince
100 g mushrooms, sliced
2 × 400 g cans tomatoes in juice,
    chopped
1 cup tomato purée
1 teaspoon oregano
½ teaspoon basil
1 teaspoon sugar
salt and freshly ground black pepper

CHEESE SAUCE

50 g butter
3 tablespoons Edmonds standard
    grade flour
1½ cups milk
¾ cup grated tasty cheddar cheese
salt
pepper

300 g packet wide lasagne, cooked
2 tablespoons freshly grated
    parmesan cheese

MEAT SAUCE

Heat oil in a large frying pan. Add onion and garlic. Cook until onion is golden. Increase heat. Add meat and brown well. Add mushrooms, tomatoes in juice, tomato purée, oregano, basil and sugar. Stir. Bring to the boil then reduce heat and simmer gently for 40 minutes or until meat mixture has thickened slightly, stirring occasionally. Season with salt and pepper to taste. Set aside until cool.

CHEESE SAUCE

Melt butter in a saucepan. Add flour and cook until frothy. Gradually add milk, stirring constantly until mixture boils and thickens. Remove from heat. Stir in cheese. Season with salt and pepper to taste. Cover with a lid or plastic wrap to prevent a skin forming. Set aside until cool.

Place half the lasagne in a greased ovenproof dish. Spread with half the meat mixture and half the cheese sauce. Repeat the layers. Top with parmesan cheese. Bake at 180°C for 20 minutes or until golden and heated through.

ITALIAN BAKED FISH » 131

136 » MARINARA

MOROCCAN LAMB AND COUSCOUS PILAF » 136

137 » MOROCCAN LAMB STEW

MARINARA

½ cup dry white wine
1 small onion, chopped
12 fresh mussels, scrubbed and
  beards removed
250 g white fish fillets (e.g. gurnard,
  tarakihi, snapper)
1 teaspoon canola oil
1 clove garlic, chopped
400 g can tomatoes in juice
¼ cup chopped parsley
100 g cooked shrimps
250 g pasta, cooked (e.g. bows,
  spaghetti)

Put wine, onion and mussels into a large frying pan. Cover and cook until mussels open. Remove mussels from shell. Discard any which do not open. Add fish to pan and gently cook for 10 minutes or until fish flakes easily. Carefully lift fish from pan, reserving all liquid. Continue cooking until liquid has reduced by half. In a separate saucepan, heat oil and garlic and cook until golden. Stir in tomatoes in juice and parsley. Bring to the boil. Add reserved fish liquid. Mash tomatoes slightly. Reduce heat and cook uncovered until sauce thickens slightly. Stir in mussels, shrimps and fish. Gently heat through. Serve over hot pasta.

MOROCCAN LAMB AND COUSCOUS PILAF

1 tablespoon Moroccan seasoning
300 g lamb fillets (about 5 fillets)
3 tablespoons pure olive oil
1 onion, finely chopped
½ cup freshly squeezed orange juice (2
  oranges)
1 cup water
1 cup couscous
1 tablespoon butter
½ cup toasted slivered almonds
½ cup chopped dried apricots
¼ cup chopped mint
¼ cup chopped coriander
¼ cup chopped parsley
salt and freshly ground black pepper
  to season

Sprinkle seasoning over lamb fillets. Heat 2 tablespoons of the oil in a heavy-based frying pan. Cook lamb for 8–9 minutes until browned all over, turning occasionally. Remove fillets from pan and cover with foil to keep warm. Add remaining oil to pan and cook onion for 4–5 minutes until soft. Remove from pan and set aside. Place orange juice and water in a saucepan. Bring to the boil. Stir in couscous. Remove from heat, cover pan and stand for 2–3 minutes until the liquid has been absorbed. Add butter and place over a very low heat for 2 minutes, stirring constantly with a fork to separate the grains. Stir in cooked onion, almonds, apricots, mint, coriander and parsley. Season. Slice lamb thinly. Toss through couscous.

MOROCCAN LAMB STEW

2 tablespoons canola oil
1 onion, sliced
2 garlic cloves, crushed
2 tablespoons Edmonds standard
  grade flour
salt and freshly ground black pepper
700 g boneless lamb, diced
2¾ cups vegetable stock
1 tablespoon tomato purée
1 lemon
2 tablespoons pitted black olives
1 red capsicum, seeded and chopped
¼ cup roughly chopped parsley
couscous to serve

Heat the oil in a large pan, and then fry the onion and garlic for 4–5 minutes until just golden. Combine flour, salt and pepper in a bowl. Coat meat in seasoned flour. Fry, turning frequently, until starting to brown. Stir in the stock and tomato purée. Bring just to the boil, then reduce the heat, cover and simmer gently for 1 hour until the meat is just tender and the sauce is slightly thickened. Slice off two strips of zest from the lemon and squeeze its juice. Stir the zest strips and juice into the stew with the olives and the red capsicum. Cook over a gentle heat for 7–8 minutes until the capsicum is just cooked. Season with salt and pepper if necessary, then stir in the parsley. Cool, transfer to a non-metallic container and cover; chill overnight. Tip the stew into a large pan and reheat gently for 20 minutes. Serve on a bed of couscous.

MOUSSAKA

1 tablespoon salt
2 large eggplants, sliced
2 tablespoons pure olive oil
2 onions, chopped
2 cloves garlic, crushed
750 g lean lamb mince
400 g can tomatoes in juice, drained
  and chopped
290 g can tomato purée
½ cup chicken stock
salt and freshly ground black pepper
¼ cup pure olive oil
2 egg yolks
1 tablespoon Edmonds standard grade
  flour
250 g natural unsweetened yoghurt
¼ cup freshly grated parmesan cheese

Sprinkle salt over eggplant and set aside for 30 minutes. Heat first measure of oil in a saucepan. Add onion and garlic and cook for 5 minutes until onion is soft. Add mince, stirring frequently, until browned. Stir in tomatoes, tomato purée and stock. Bring to the boil. Reduce heat, cover and simmer gently for 30 minutes. Season to taste with salt and pepper. Rinse eggplant slices under cold running water. Drain and pat dry with paper towels. Heat second measure of oil in a frying pan. Fry eggplant until light brown and soft. Place one-third of the eggplant in an ovenproof dish. Spread with half the meat mixture. Top with another third of eggplant and repeat with meat, finishing with eggplant. In a bowl, combine egg yolks, flour and yoghurt. Season with salt and pepper. Spread on top of eggplant. Top with parmesan cheese. Bake at 180°C for 40 minutes or until golden.

MOUSSAKA ◈ 137

139 ◈ MUSSELS IN TOMATO SAUCE

PASTA WITH PESTO, CRISPY
BACON AND WALNUTS ◈ 139

139 ◈ PENNE PASTA WITH BROCCOLI
AND BLUE CHEESE SAUCE

MUSSELS IN TOMATO SAUCE

SERVES 4–6

1 onion, chopped
1 cup dry white wine
36 mussels, scrubbed and beards
  removed
1 tablespoon butter
2 cloves garlic, crushed
1 tablespoon Edmonds standard grade
  flour
290 g can tomato purée
2 tablespoons chopped parsley
freshly ground black pepper

Put half the onion in a large frying pan. Add wine and bring to the boil. Add mussels. Cover and cook for about 8 minutes, until mussels open, removing them as they do. Discard any that do not open. Remove from heat. Drain, reserving ¾ cup of cooking liquid. Keep mussels warm. Melt butter in a saucepan. Add remaining onion and garlic. Cook for 5 minutes until onion is soft. Add flour and stir over a medium heat for 2 minutes. Remove from heat. Gradually add tomato purée and reserved cooking liquid. Return to heat, stirring constantly until sauce thickens and comes to the boil. Boil for 1 minute. Stir in parsley. Season to taste with pepper. Pour sauce over mussels. Serve with crusty French bread.

PASTA WITH PESTO, CRISPY BACON AND WALNUTS

SERVES 4

400 g fettuccine
pure olive oil
6 rashers lean rindless bacon, roughly
  chopped
½ cup Pesto (see page 227)
2 tablespoons pure olive oil
¾ cup walnut pieces, toasted
½ cup freshly grated parmesan cheese
freshly ground black pepper to season
basil and parmesan cheese to garnish

Cook pasta according to packet instructions. Pour a little olive oil into a frying pan and heat. Cook bacon for 8–10 minutes until crisp and brown. Drain cooked pasta in a sieve. Return to saucepan and toss through all ingredients. Serve immediately. Garnish with sprigs of basil and parmesan cheese shavings.

PENNE PASTA WITH BROCCOLI AND BLUE CHEESE SAUCE

SERVES 4

500 g penne pasta
1 tablespoon pure olive oil
1 onion, chopped
2 cloves garlic, crushed
1 head broccoli, cut into florets
300 ml cream
100 g blue cheese, crumbled
salt and freshly ground black pepper

Cook pasta according to instructions on the packet. While the pasta is cooking, prepare the sauce. Heat oil in a frying pan. Cook onion for 5 minutes until soft. Add garlic and broccoli and cook for 3–4 minutes until broccoli is tender but still crunchy. Combine cream and cheese in a saucepan. Stir over a low heat until cheese melts and sauce is smooth. Stir in broccoli mixture. Drain pasta. Toss sauce through pasta. Season to taste. Serve with a tossed salad and fresh bread.

PESTO AND BLUE CHEESE RIGATI

400 g rigati pasta
2 tablespoons pure olive oil
1 onion, sliced
2 cloves garlic, crushed
¼ cup Pesto (see page 227)
200 g blue cheese, crumbled
freshly ground black pepper to season
shavings of parmesan cheese to
    garnish (optional)

Cook pasta according to instructions on the packet. While pasta is cooking, heat oil in a frying pan. Cook onion and garlic for 5 minutes until soft. Stir in Pesto. Toss onion mixture, cheese and pepper through the cooked, drained pasta. Divide between four serving plates. Garnish with parmesan shavings.

PORK AND NOODLE STIR-FRY

500 g lean pork schnitzel
3 tablespoons hoisin sauce
¼ cup soy sauce
1 tablespoon honey
2 teaspoons crushed garlic
225 g dried egg noodles
2 tablespoons canola oil
2 onions, thinly sliced
½ cup water
2 bunches bok choy, sliced
1 tablespoon Edmonds Fielder's
    cornflour
1 tablespoon water

Cut pork into 1 cm wide strips. Combine hoisin sauce, soy sauce, honey and garlic in a bowl. Add pork and toss to combine. Cover and refrigerate for 1 hour. Cook noodles according to packet instructions. Tip into a sieve and refresh under cold running water. Heat 1 tablespoon of the oil in a wok or heavy-based frying pan. Drain meat from marinade, reserving the marinade. Stir-fry meat for 4–5 minutes until cooked through. Remove from wok. Add remaining oil to wok. Stir-fry onion for 4–5 minutes until soft. Combine reserved marinade and water and add to wok. Add pork, cooked noodles and bok choy, tossing over a medium heat for 1–2 minutes until heated through. Mix cornflour to a paste with water. Add to wok, stirring until mixture thickens. Serve immediately.

NOTE: Shanghai choy may be used instead of bok choy.

PESTO AND BLUE CHEESE RIGATI ◆ 140

140 ◆ PORK AND NOODLE STIR-FRY

PORK AND SPINACH RISOTTO ◆ 143

143 ◆ PUMPKIN AND LEEK RISOTTO

QUICK THAI GREEN CHICKEN CURRY ◈ 144

144 ◈ RACK OF LAMB WITH A ROSEMARY CRUST

ROAST LAMB WITH FRESH MINT CHUTNEY ◈ 144

145 ◈ ROAST STUFFED CHICKEN

PORK AND SPINACH RISOTTO

1 pork fillet, approximately 350 g
2 tablespoons soy sauce
1 tablespoon dry sherry
1 tablespoon liquid honey
2 teaspoons sweet chilli sauce
1.5 litres beef stock, approximately
¼ cup pure olive oil
1 onion, finely sliced
1 teaspoon crushed garlic
500 g Arborio rice
1 cup dry white wine
1 tablespoon pure olive oil
2 cups shredded spinach
½ cup freshly grated parmesan cheese
salt and freshly ground black pepper
   to season

Trim visible fat from pork fillet. Place in a shallow glass or ceramic dish. Combine soy sauce, sherry, honey and chilli sauce. Pour over pork. Turn to coat evenly. Cover and refrigerate for at least 1 hour or up to 8 hours. Bring stock to the boil in a saucepan. Heat first measure of oil in a heavy-based, deep-sided frying pan. Cook onion for 5 minutes until soft. Add garlic and rice and stir over a low heat for 2–3 minutes to toast the rice. Add wine and cook for 1 minute. Ladle over sufficient boiling stock to just cover the rice. Cook, stirring frequently, adding more stock to cover the rice as the liquid is absorbed. This will take about 18 minutes. While rice is cooking, heat second measure of oil in a heavy-based frying pan. Drain pork from marinade. Cook meat over a medium-high heat, turning frequently, for about 12 minutes until cooked through. Remove from heat and allow meat to rest for 5 minutes before slicing thinly. Remove risotto pan from the heat. Add spinach, parmesan and sliced pork. Stir to combine. Cover pan and stand for 3–4 minutes. Season. Pile onto warm serving plates.

PUMPKIN AND LEEK RISOTTO

2 tablespoons butter
2 tablespoons pure olive oil
250 g peeled, seeded pumpkin, cut
   into 1 cm cubes
1 small leek, sliced and washed
1 teaspoon crushed garlic
1.5 litres chicken or vegetable stock,
   approximately
2 tablespoons pure olive oil
500 g Arborio rice
½ cup dry white wine
½ cup freshly grated parmesan cheese
2 tablespoons chopped parsley
salt and freshly ground black pepper
   to taste

Combine butter and first measure of oil in a frying pan. Heat until butter melts. Add pumpkin, leek and garlic. Stir over a low heat for 2–3 minutes. Cover pan and continue cooking for 10–12 minutes, stirring occasionally, until pumpkin is tender. While vegetables are cooking, heat stock to boiling point in a saucepan. Heat second measure of oil in a heavy-based, deep-sided frying pan. Add rice to frying pan and stir over a low heat for 2–3 minutes to toast. Add wine and cook for 1 minute. Ladle over sufficient boiling stock to just cover the rice. Cook, stirring frequently, adding more stock to cover the rice as the liquid is absorbed. This will take about 18 minutes. Remove pan from the heat. Add cooked vegetables, parmesan and parsley. Stir gently to combine. Cover pan and stand for 3–4 minutes. Season. Pile onto warm serving plates.

QUICK THAI GREEN CHICKEN CURRY

SERVES 4

2 tablespoons Thai green curry paste
1 onion, thinly sliced
750 g boneless skinless chicken,
    thinly sliced
1 cup coconut cream
1 tablespoon fish sauce
2 spring onions, thinly sliced
2 courgettes, thinly sliced
¼ teaspoon finely chopped, seeded
    red chilli
2 tablespoons roughly chopped
    coriander
cooked rice to serve

Heat a medium, heavy-based frying pan. Add curry paste and onion and cook for 1–2 minutes, stirring constantly, until paste is fragrant. Add chicken and cook for 4–5 minutes, stirring frequently. Add coconut cream and fish sauce and cook for a further 3–4 minutes, until chicken is cooked through. Stir through spring onions, courgettes, chilli and coriander. Serve immediately on a bed of cooked rice.

RACK OF LAMB WITH A ROSEMARY CRUST

SERVES 4

½ cup dry breadcrumbs
2 tablespoons finely chopped
    rosemary
2 cloves garlic, crushed
salt and freshly ground black pepper
    to season
¼ cup melted butter
2 racks lamb, each with 6 cutlets

Combine breadcrumbs, rosemary, garlic, salt, pepper and butter in a bowl. Mix well. Trim any excess fat from lamb racks. Spread crumb mixture over the fatty surface of the lamb racks, pressing firmly. Place lamb racks, crust-side up, in a roasting dish. Bake at 200°C for 25–30 minutes or until the meat is cooked to the desired level. Cover with foil and stand for 10 minutes before slicing into cutlets.

ROAST LAMB WITH FRESH MINT CHUTNEY

SERVES 4–6

1 kg shank end leg of lamb
3 cloves garlic
8 strips lemon zest

FRESH MINT CHUTNEY
2 spring onions
1 clove garlic
1 cup firmly packed mint leaves
½ teaspoon salt
1 teaspoon sugar
1 teaspoon garam masala
¼ cup lemon juice
1 teaspoon prepared minced chilli

Remove skin from lamb, leaving a thin layer of fat. Crush garlic, peel and cut into slivers. Cut slashes in lamb fat and push a garlic sliver in each. Arrange lemon zest over. Bake at 180°C for 1½ hours for medium-rare lamb or until preferred doneness. Serve sliced, accompanied by Fresh Mint Chutney.

FRESH MINT CHUTNEY
Trim spring onions and chop roughly. Crush and peel garlic. Place spring onions, garlic, mint, salt, sugar, garam masala, lemon juice and prepared minced chilli into a food processor or blender. Process until smooth.

ROAST STUFFED CHICKEN

1 no. 8 chicken

BASIC BREAD STUFFING
3 cups soft breadcrumbs
1 onion, finely chopped
1 teaspoon dried sage
2 tablespoons melted butter
1 egg
salt
pepper

Remove giblets from chicken. Use to make stock. To make stuffing, combine breadcrumbs, onion, sage, butter and egg in bowl. Season with salt and pepper to taste. Spoon the stuffing into the cavity of the bird and secure opening with skewers. Bake 180°C for 1 hour or until juices run clear.

SAUSAGE-MEAT STUFFING
Add 200g sausage meat to half a quantity of basic stuffing.

ORANGE AND ROSEMARY STUFFING
Add 2 tablespoons grated orange zest and 2 teaspoons rosemary.

APRICOT STUFFING
Add ½ cup chopped dried apricots, which have been soaked in ¼ cup orange juice for 2 hours.

SALMON CAKES WITH PARSLEY SAUCE

450 g potatoes
210 g can pink salmon
2 tablespoons butter
4 spring onions, chopped
1 tablespoon lemon juice
1 tablespoon chopped parsley
1 cup Edmonds standard grade flour
salt and freshly ground black pepper
1 egg, beaten
1 cup fresh white breadcrumbs
2 tablespoons canola oil
1 cup Parsley Sauce (see page 227)
  to serve

Peel potatoes, cut into evenly-sized pieces and cook in boiling salted water until tender. Drain well and mash until smooth. Drain salmon and flake, removing any skin and bones. Mix fish with potato. Melt butter in a small saucepan. Add spring onions and cook until they begin to soften. Add to fish mixture with lemon juice, parsley and flour. Season to taste with salt and pepper. Add just enough beaten egg to bind mixture. It must be firm enough to shape into cakes. With floured hands, shape mixture into eight cakes. Brush with beaten egg and coat in breadcrumbs. Chill for 30 minutes. Heat oil in a frying pan and shallow-fry fish cakes (in batches, if necessary) for about 5 minutes on each side until golden and crisp. Drain on kitchen paper. Serve immediately with Parsley Sauce.

SALMON STEAKS WITH THAI DIPPING SAUCE

SERVES 6

1 teaspoon sesame oil
2 tablespoons lime or lemon juice
4 salmon steaks

THAI DIPPING SAUCE
1 clove garlic
¼ cup white vinegar
1 tablespoon raw sugar
½ teaspoon salt
½ teaspoon prepared minced chilli
2 teaspoons finely chopped fresh
    coriander

Mix sesame oil and lime or lemon juice together.
Brush over one side of salmon. Grill for
2 minutes. Turn and brush second side with lime
mixture. Grill for 2 minutes or until salmon is
just cooked. Serve with Thai Dipping Sauce.

THAI DIPPING SAUCE
Crush, peel and finely chop garlic. Mix garlic,
vinegar, sugar, salt, chilli and coriander together.

SHEPHERD'S PIE

SERVES 4

1 tablespoon canola oil
1 onion, chopped
500 g mince
2 tablespoons Edmonds standard
    grade flour
1 tablespoon tomato sauce
1 tablespoon chutney or relish
¾ cup beef stock
3 potatoes, peeled and chopped
1 tablespoon butter
1 tablespoon finely chopped onion
½ cup grated tasty cheddar cheese
salt
black pepper

Heat oil in a large frying pan. Add onion and
cook until clear. Add mince and cook until well
browned, stirring constantly. Pour off excess
fat. Stir in flour and cook for 1 minute. Add
tomato sauce, chutney and stock. Bring to the
boil, reduce heat and simmer for 5 minutes. Set
aside. Cook potatoes in boiling, salted water until
tender. Drain and heat for a few minutes to dry
off excess moisture. Shake the pan frequently
during this time. Mash potato. Add butter, onion
and half the cheese, mixing until smooth and
creamy. Season with salt and pepper to taste. Put
mince into a pie dish. Top with potato mixture.
Sprinkle with remaining cheese. Bake at 180°C
for 20 minutes or until golden and heated
through.

SALMON CAKES WITH PARSLEY SAUCE ⦁ 145

SPICED CHICKEN PILAF ⬥ 150

150 ⬥ SPINACH AND BACON SAUCE

SUNDRIED TOMATO AND FETA-
STUFFED CHICKEN BREASTS ⬥ 151

152 ⬥ SWEET AND SOUR PORK

SMOKED SALMON PASTA SAUCE

200 g wood-roasted salmon
1 small onion
1 clove garlic
1 teaspoon canola oil
1 teaspoon prepared whole seed
   mustard
1 tablespoon chopped parsley
1 tablespoon chopped fresh dill
1 tablespoon chopped fresh chives
1 cup natural unsweetened yoghurt
500 g egg fettucine

Remove skin from salmon and flake flesh. Peel onion and chop finely. Crush, peel and chop garlic. Heat oil and sauté onion and garlic for 5 minutes or until clear. Add salmon, mustard, parsley, dill, chives and yoghurt. Bring to the boil and then reduce heat. Cook pasta to packet directions. Drain. Toss through smoked salmon sauce.

SPANISH PAELLA

6 cups fish or chicken stock
400 g can whole tomatoes in juice
pinch of saffron threads
1 single boneless chicken breast
1 pork fillet
2 onions
2 cloves garlic
1 green pepper
3 tablespoons pure olive oil
3 cups short-grain rice
12 mussels in shells
6 whole uncooked prawns
4 lemons

Heat the stock, tomatoes and juice and saffron threads until boiling. Remove skin from chicken breast and discard. Cut chicken into 1 cm strips. Cut pork fillet into 1 cm cubes. Peel onions and chop coarsely. Crush, peel and finely chop garlic. Remove core from green pepper and cut flesh into 1 cm cubes. Heat oil in a paella dish or large frying pan. Sauté chicken and pork until lightly browned. Add onions and pepper and sauté for 2 minutes. Add rice and stir to coat. Cook until rice becomes transparent. Add the hot stock mixture and stir. Simmer for 10 minutes. Add mussels and simmer for 5 minutes or until mussels open. Discard any that do not open. Add prawns and cook for a further 2 minutes. Add more stock if necessary. Remove from heat. Squeeze the juice of two of the lemons over the top of the paella. Cover and stand for 5 minutes. Cut remaining lemons into quarters and use to garnish paella.

SPICED CHICKEN PILAF

2 single boneless skinless chicken
  breasts
1 tablespoon canola oil
1 onion, finely chopped
2 cloves garlic, crushed
1½ cups basmati rice, thoroughly
  washed
2½ cups chicken stock
½ cup freshly squeezed orange juice
  (2 oranges)
1 teaspoon turmeric
½ teaspoon ground cinnamon
2 bay leaves
3 spring onions, chopped
½ cup toasted sliced almonds
2 tablespoons chopped parsley
salt and freshly ground black pepper
  to season

Cut chicken into bite-sized pieces. Heat oil in a heavy-based frying pan. Cook chicken and onion for about 5 minutes until onion is soft. Add garlic, rice, stock, orange juice, turmeric, cinnamon and bay leaves. Bring to the boil, stirring frequently. Reduce heat to low. Cover pan and simmer for about 20–25 minutes, stirring occasionally, until rice is cooked and the liquid is absorbed. Remove from heat. Remove bay leaves. Add spring onions, almonds and parsley. Stir to combine. Season to taste.

SPINACH AND BACON SAUCE

1 tablespoon butter
1 onion, chopped
1 clove garlic, crushed
4 rashers bacon, chopped
2–3 bunches spinach, chopped
250 g pasta, cooked (e.g. spirals,
  spaghetti)

Melt butter in a large frying pan. Add onion, garlic and bacon. Cook until onion is clear and bacon is cooked. Stir in spinach and cook for a further 2 minutes or until spinach is a rich, dark green colour, stirring constantly. Serve over hot pasta.

SQUID RINGS

500 g squid rings
2 cloves garlic, crushed
2 eggs
1 tablespoon Edmonds Fielder's
  cornflour
1 tablespoon milk
2 cups toasted breadcrumbs,
  approximately
canola oil for deep-frying

Put squid and garlic in a bowl. Leave for 15 minutes. Beat eggs, cornflour and milk together. Dip squid rings into egg mixture. Coat with breadcrumbs. Deep-fry in hot oil for 2 minutes or until golden. Do not overcook as this will toughen the squid. Serve with a dipping sauce.

STIR-FRIED LEMON AND GINGER FISH

SERVES 4

4 medium fish fillets, skinned and
  boned
1 medium onion
1 tablespoon peanut oil
1 tablespoon grated root ginger
1 tablespoon Edmonds Fielder's
  cornflour
¼ cup lemon juice
1 teaspoon grated lemon zest
1 cup chicken stock
1 tablespoon brown sugar
chopped spring onion greens

Cut fish into 2 cm wide strips, about 6 cm long. Peel onion and cut into eighths. Heat oil in a wok or heavy frying pan and stir-fry onion and ginger for 2 minutes. Add fish and stir-fry for 2 minutes or until fish is almost cooked. Mix cornflour and lemon juice together until smooth. Add lemon zest, stock and brown sugar. Pour over fish. Bring to the boil and cook for 1 minute. Serve garnished with spring onion greens.

SUNDRIED TOMATO AND FETA-STUFFED CHICKEN BREASTS

SERVES 4

1 cup fresh white breadcrumbs
200 g feta cheese, crumbled
⅓ cup chopped sundried tomatoes
2 spring onions, sliced
1 tablespoon chopped rosemary
1 egg
salt and freshly ground black pepper
  to season
4 single boneless skinless chicken
  breasts
12 rashers streaky rindless bacon
liquid honey to drizzle

To make the stuffing, combine breadcrumbs, feta, sundried tomatoes, spring onions, rosemary, egg and salt and pepper in a bowl. Mix well. Trim visible fat from chicken. Place chicken between two sheets of plastic wrap. Pound with a heavy object (e.g. a rolling pin) to flatten to an even thickness of 6 mm. Cover half of each breast with stuffing, then fold over to enclose. Wrap three rashers of bacon around each parcel to cover. Place chicken in a baking dish. Drizzle over a little honey. Bake at 180°C for 25–30 minutes, basting chicken once or twice during this time. Turn oven to grill for 2–3 minutes to crisp the bacon. Stand for 4–5 minutes before cutting parcels into slices. Arrange slices of chicken on serving plates. Serve with vegetables of your choice, or a tossed salad.

SWEET AND SOUR PORK

500 g pork pieces
2 cloves garlic, crushed
2 tablespoons canola oil
2 small onions, quartered
½ cup chicken stock
225 g can pineapple pieces in juice
1 tablespoon Edmonds Fielder's
    cornflour
¼ cup tomato sauce
½ teaspoon grated root ginger
2 tablespoons white vinegar
2 tablespoons brown sugar
½ cup chopped red pepper
½ cup chopped cucumber
½ cup baby sweetcorn
100 g mushrooms, quartered

Trim fat from pork and cut into 2 cm pieces. Peel garlic and chop finely. Heat oil in a saucepan or wok. Add onion and garlic and cook until onion is clear. Remove from pan. Add half the pork pieces and quickly brown on all sides. Remove from pan. Repeat with remaining meat. Return meat and onions to pan. Add stock and bring to the boil. Cover and cook gently for 30 minutes or until meat is tender. Drain pineapple, reserving juice. Combine juice and cornflour, mixing until smooth. Add pineapple pieces, tomato sauce, ginger, vinegar, sugar, pepper, cucumber, sweetcorn and mushrooms to pan. Cook for 5 minutes. Return to the boil. Stir in cornflour mixture and boil for 2 minutes or until mixture thickens slightly. Serve with rice or noodles.

TANDOORI CHICKEN BREASTS

¾ cup natural unsweetened yoghurt
2 cloves garlic, crushed
1 tablespoon lemon juice
2 teaspoons grated root ginger
2 tablespoons paprika
1 teaspoon ground cumin
½ teaspoon ground cardamom
¼ teaspoon chilli powder
4 single boneless skinless chicken
    breasts
cooked rice, naan or papadums to
    serve
mango chutney to serve
Cucumber and Mint Raita (see page
    226) to serve

Combine yoghurt, garlic, lemon juice, ginger, paprika, cumin, cardamom and chilli powder in a bowl. Mix well. Trim visible fat from chicken. Place chicken between two sheets of plastic wrap. Pound with a heavy object (e.g. a rolling pin) until chicken is an even thickness — about 1 cm thick. Preheat oven grill. Place chicken in a single layer in a shallow roasting dish. Smother upper surface of chicken with half of the tandoori mixture. Grill for 6–8 minutes. Turn chicken and smother remaining side with tandoori mixture. Grill for a further 6–8 minutes until cooked through. Serve on a bed of cooked rice, accompanied by naan or papadums, mango chutney and Cucumber and Mint Raita.

THAI FISH CAKES

MAKES 26

185 g can tuna in brine
1 teaspoon ground coriander
1 teaspoon Thai fish sauce
¼ cup coconut cream
1 egg
2 tablespoons chopped fresh coriander
1 teaspoon prepared minced chilli
1½ cups soft breadcrumbs
½ teaspoon salt
¼ cup peanut oil

Drain tuna. Place tuna, coriander, fish sauce, coconut cream, egg, fresh coriander, chilli, breadcrumbs and salt in a food processor. Process until combined but not paste-like. Measure tablespoonsful of mixture and cook in hot oil in a frying pan until golden on both sides. Drain on absorbent paper and serve hot.

THAI-STYLE BEEF AND BABY CORN STIR-FRY

SERVES 4

500 g lean fast-fry beef steak (e.g. rump, porterhouse or fillet)
2 tablespoons canola oil
1 teaspoon crushed garlic
1 small red chilli, seeded and finely chopped
2 teaspoons Thai-style red curry paste
2 tablespoons fish sauce
2 tablespoons oyster sauce
2 × 425 g cans baby corn, drained
salt and freshly ground black pepper
¾ cup roasted peanuts
2 tablespoons chopped coriander

Cut meat into narrow strips. Heat oil in wok or large heavy-based frying pan. Stir-fry beef, garlic and chilli over a high heat for 3–4 minutes. Add curry paste, fish sauce, oyster sauce and corn. Stir-fry for 2–3 minutes. Season with salt and pepper. Add peanuts and coriander and toss to combine. Serve on a bed of cooked rice.

VEAL CORDON BLEU

SERVES 4

8 small pieces wiener schnitzel
2 large slices ham
4 slices mozzarella cheese
½ cup Edmonds standard grade flour
salt
pepper
2 eggs
¼ cup water
1½ cups toasted breadcrumbs
50 g butter
2 tablespoons canola oil

Put a piece of plastic wrap over one schnitzel at a time. Using a rolling pin, roll the meat thinner. Repeat with remaining meat. Cut ham in half. On half the pieces of meat, place a piece of ham, top with a slice of cheese. Place another piece of meat on top, pressing edges together. Combine flour, salt and pepper to taste. Coat schnitzels in seasoned flour. Beat eggs and water together. Dip schnitzels in this. Coat in breadcrumbs. Repeat with egg and breadcrumbs. Heat butter and oil together in a large frying pan. Add schnitzel and cook for 5 minutes each side or until golden.

CHICKEN CORDON BLEU
Use boneless chicken breasts instead of veal schnitzel. Roll thinly then proceed as above.

PIZZAS GALORE
PIZZA DOUGH

1 tablespoon Edmonds active yeast
½ teaspoon sugar
1 cup tepid water
1 teaspoon salt
3 cups Edmonds high grade flour
1 tablespoon pure olive oil

Combine yeast, sugar and water in a bowl. Set aside for 15 minutes or until frothy. Combine salt and flour in a large bowl. Add yeast mixture and oil. Mix to a soft dough. Transfer to a lightly floured surface and knead for 5 minutes, until smooth and elastic. Place dough in a lightly oiled large bowl and cover with a teatowel. Stand in a warm place until doubled in bulk. Punch dough down in the centre, knead lightly for 1 minute and roll into a 30 cm round circle. Place on a lightly greased oven tray. Top with ingredients of your choice. Bake at 220°C for 15 minutes or until well risen and golden.

NOTE: To cook pizza on a pizza stone, transfer completed uncooked pizza to a heated pizza stone and cook as above.

TOMATO SAUCE

1 tablespoon pure olive oil
1 onion, finely chopped
1 teaspoon crushed garlic
400 g can tomatoes in juice
2 tablespoons tomato paste
1 tablespoon chopped basil
salt and freshly ground black pepper

Heat oil in a frying pan. Cook onion for 5 minutes until soft. Add garlic, tomatoes and tomato paste, breaking up the tomatoes with a wooden spoon. Simmer for about 20 minutes until sauce is thick. Stir in basil. Season to taste.

TOPPING COMBINATIONS FOR PIZZAS

PIZZA SUPREME
Spread the prepared pizza base with Tomato Sauce. Top with sliced salami, diced ham, anchovies, strips of roasted red capsicum, halved button mushrooms, pitted halved olives, thinly sliced red onion and grated mozzarella cheese.

GREEK PIZZA
Spread the prepared pizza base with Tomato Sauce. Top with diced feta cheese, pitted halved olives, thinly sliced red onion, strips of roasted red capsicum and grated mozzarella cheese.

VEGETARIAN PIZZA
Spread the prepared pizza base with Pesto (see page 227). Top with roasted sliced eggplant, thinly sliced red onion, crumbled feta cheese, sliced cherry tomatoes and a scattering of grated mozzarella cheese.

CHICKEN AND BLUE CHEESE PIZZA
Spread the prepared pizza base with Pesto (see page 227). Top with a little grated cheddar cheese, shredded cooked chicken, crumbled blue cheese, chopped walnuts and halved cherry tomatoes.

TOMATO SAUCE ⬗ 155 PIZZA SUPREME, VEGETARIAN AND GREEK PIZZA ⬗ 156

BACON-WRAPPED SAUSAGES ✳ HONEY AND THYME
MARINATED CHICKEN BREASTS ✳ GARLIC AND SWEET
CHILLI PRAWNS ✳ BARBECUED VEGETABLES ✳ 158

BARBECUE BONANZA

BACON-WRAPPED SAUSAGES

8 quality sausages
8 rashers rindless bacon
wholegrain mustard to spread

Prick each sausage with a fork. Lay bacon on a flat surface. Spread each rasher with a little mustard. Wrap a rasher around each sausage. Cook on a preheated barbecue for 12–15 minutes until cooked through, turning occasionally.

BARBECUED VEGETABLES

½ cup pure olive oil
1 teaspoon crushed garlic
4 capsicums (any colour)
4 small courgettes
1 small eggplant
2 red onions
8 flat mushrooms

Combine oil and garlic. Prepare vegetables. Halve capsicums, remove core and seeds. Cut each half into three pieces. Trim courgettes. Cut in half lengthwise. Trim ends off eggplant. Cut into 1 cm thick rounds. Peel onions. Cut into quarters. Brush vegetables liberally all over with the oil. Cook on a preheated barbecue until tender. Serve with Sundried Tomato Pesto (see page 221).

GARLIC AND SWEET CHILLI PRAWNS

2 tablespoons lemon juice
2 tablespoons sweet chilli sauce
2 tablespoons chopped coriander
1 tablespoon pure olive oil
2 cloves garlic, crushed
24 uncooked king prawns
lemon wedges to garnish

Combine lemon juice, chilli sauce, coriander, oil and garlic in a medium bowl. Add prawns and mix well. Cover and refrigerate for 2 hours. Cook on a preheated barbecue for 4–5 minutes until cooked through, turning once. Transfer to a serving plate. Garnish with lemon wedges.

HONEY AND THYME MARINATED CHICKEN BREASTS

SERVES 4

2 tablespoons white vinegar
2 tablespoons pure olive oil
2 tablespoons soy sauce
2 tablespoons honey
2 tablespoons tomato purée
2 cloves garlic, crushed
2 teaspoons finely chopped thyme
4 single boneless skinless chicken
   breasts (or chicken portions)

Combine all ingredients except chicken. Mix well. Place chicken breasts between two sheets of plastic wrap. Using a heavy object, pound to an even thickness of about 1 cm. Place in a single layer in a glass or ceramic dish. Pour over marinade and turn to coat. Leave to marinate in the refrigerator for at least 1 hour. Cook over a medium heat on a preheated barbecue for 8–10 minutes until cooked through, turning once.

DESSERTS

APPLE PIE ◆ 161

161 ◆ APPLE STRUDEL

BAKED LEMON CHEESECAKE ◆ 161

162 ◆ BANANA PANCAKES

APPLE PIE

200 g Sweet Shortcrust Pastry
(see page 224) or 200 g Edmonds
sweet short pastry
25 g butter, melted
milk or water
2 teaspoons sugar

FILLING
4–6 Granny Smith apples
½ cup sugar
2 tablespoons Edmonds standard
grade flour
¼ teaspoon ground cloves

On a lightly floured board, roll out pastry slightly larger than a 20 cm pie plate. Cut two 2.5 cm wide strips long enough to go around the edge of the pie plate. Brush with water. Spoon apple filling into centre of pie plate. Pour butter over filling. Cover with remaining pastry. Press edges firmly together to seal. Cut steam holes in centre of pastry. Trim and crimp edges. Decorate pie with any pastry trimmings. Brush lightly with milk or water. Sprinkle with sugar. Bake at 200°C for 25 minutes or until pastry is golden. Test with a skewer if the apple is cooked. If not, reduce oven temperature to 180°C and cook until apple is tender.

FILLING
Peel, core and slice the apples. Combine sugar, flour and cloves. Toss apples in this mixture.

APPLE STRUDEL

6 sheets Edmonds filo pastry
½ cup soft breadcrumbs
567 g can spiced apples
½ cup sultanas
1 tablespoon melted butter
icing sugar

Layer filo sheets on greased baking tray, sprinkling breadcrumbs between each. Keep remaining filo sheets under a damp teatowel as you work. Mix apples and sultanas together. Spread over half of the pastry to within 5 cm from edge. Wet pastry edges. Fold pastry over filling and seal edges. Cut three slashes in top of pastry. Brush with butter. Bake at 200°C for 25 minutes or until pastry is golden. Dust with icing sugar and serve warm or cold.

BAKED LEMON CHEESECAKE

125 g malt biscuits
50 g butter
4 eggs
250 g sour cream
250 g plain cottage cheese
4 teaspoons grated lemon zest
2 tablespoons lemon juice
½ cup caster sugar

Crush biscuits. Melt butter. Mix biscuit crumbs and butter together and press into the bottom of a 20 cm loose-bottom tin lined with baking paper. Bake at 180°C for 10 minutes. Place eggs, sour cream, cottage cheese, lemon zest, lemon juice and caster sugar in a food processor or blender and process until smooth. Pour into cooked base. Bake at 150°C for 1 hour or until cheesecake is set. Serve warm or cold.

BANANA PANCAKES

1 cup Edmonds standard grade flour
½ teaspoon ground nutmeg
⅛ teaspoon salt
1 egg
about 1 cup milk
1 large banana, mashed
sliced banana to garnish
maple syrup to serve

Sift flour, nutmeg and salt into a bowl. Add egg, mixing to combine. Gradually beat in sufficient milk to mix to a smooth batter. Chill for 1 hour. Stir. The batter will thicken on standing. Stir in banana. Heat a greased pancake pan or small frying pan. Pour in just enough batter to cover base of pan. Cook until golden on underside. Release with knife around edges. Flip or turn and cook other side. Stack pancakes as you cook. To serve, fold pancakes into quarters. Place two pancakes on each serving plate. Garnish with sliced banana and drizzle with maple syrup.

CASSATA

1 litre chocolate ice cream
½ teaspoon vanilla essence
300 ml cream
2 tablespoons icing sugar
½ cup toasted almonds
½ cup chopped dark chocolate
1 cup chopped glacé fruit

Soften ice cream and mix in vanilla essence. Use to line the base and sides of a 1 litre pudding basin. Freeze until firm. Whip cream until stiff. Fold in icing sugar, almonds, chocolate and glacé fruit. Use to fill the chocolate ice cream cavity. Cover with foil and freeze until firm. Unmould onto a serving plate by dipping bowl into hot water two or three times, then inverting onto a plate and shaking sharply. Cut into wedges to serve.

CHILLED CHEESECAKE

BASE
250 g packet digestive biscuits
1 teaspoon grated lemon zest
1 tablespoon lemon juice
75 g butter, melted

FILLING
2 teaspoons gelatine
2 tablespoons water
250 g cream cheese
250 g sour cream
½ cup sugar
2 tablespoons lemon juice
1 teaspoon grated lemon zest
1 teaspoon vanilla essence

BASE
Finely crush biscuits. Combine biscuit crumbs, lemon zest, juice and butter. Line the base and sides of a 20 cm springform tin with biscuit mixture. Chill while preparing filling.

FILLING
Combine gelatine and water. Leave to swell for 10 minutes. Beat cream cheese until soft. Add sour cream and beat until well combined. Add sugar, lemon juice, zest and vanilla essence. Beat until sugar has dissolved. Dissolve gelatine over hot water. Stir through cheese mixture. Pour filling into prepared base. Chill until set.

CASSATA ⟫ 162

162 ⟪ CHILLED CHEESECAKE

CHOCOLATE BROWNIES ⟫ 164

165 ⟪ CHOCOLATE FUDGE SELF-SAUCING PUDDING

CHOCOLATE AND ALMOND STUFFED PEACHES

6 firm ripe peaches
¼ cup freshly squeezed orange juice
   (1 orange)
100 g amaretti biscuits, crushed
¼ cup ground almonds
75 g dark chocolate, finely chopped
2 tablespoons melted butter
whipped cream or crème fraîche
   to serve

Cut peaches in half. Remove stones. Use 2 tablespoons of the orange juice to brush cut surfaces of peaches. Combine remaining orange juice with biscuit crumbs, almonds, chocolate and butter. Mix well. Pile mixture into peach cavities. Place on a baking tray. Bake at 200°C for 20 minutes until peaches are tender. Serve with whipped cream.

NOTE: Gingernuts can be used as an alternative to amaretti biscuits.

CHOCOLATE BROWNIES

250 g butter, chopped
200 g dark chocolate, chopped
2 cups sugar
4 eggs, lightly beaten
1 teaspoon vanilla essence
1 cup Edmonds standard grade flour
½ teaspoon Edmonds baking powder
½ cup cocoa
icing sugar to dust (optional)
vanilla ice cream or whipped cream
   to serve

Combine butter and chocolate in a saucepan. Stir constantly over a low heat until melted and smooth. Remove from heat and transfer mixture to a large bowl. Stir in sugar. Add eggs and vanilla essence and beat with a wooden spoon until combined. Sift flour, baking powder and cocoa. Stir into chocolate mixture. Transfer to a greased 25 × 20 cm baking tin that has the base lined with baking paper. Bake at 180°C for about 50 minutes or until firm to touch, with cracks appearing on the surface. Cool in tin. Turn onto a chopping board. Trim off edges and cut into triangles. Arrange on serving plates. If desired, dust with icing sugar. Serve with ice cream or whipped cream.

CHOCOLATE DESSERT CAKE

SERVES 6–8

1 cup seedless raisins
1 cup water
½ cup freshly squeezed orange juice
　(2 oranges)
1 teaspoon Edmonds baking soda
125 g butter, softened
¾ cup caster sugar
2 eggs
1 cup Edmonds standard grade flour
1 teaspoon Edmonds baking powder
½ cup cocoa

CHOCOLATE SAUCE
100 g dark chocolate, chopped
½ cup cream
2 tablespoons butter

orange zest to garnish

Combine raisins, water and orange juice in a small saucepan. Bring to the boil over a low heat. Remove from heat. Stir in baking soda. Cool slightly. Transfer to a food processor and blend to a smooth consistency. Cream butter and sugar until light and fluffy. Add eggs one at a time. Sift together flour, baking powder and cocoa. Fold dry ingredients and liquid ingredients alternately into creamed mixture. Transfer to a greased 22 cm round cake tin that has the base lined with baking paper. Bake at 180°C for 50–55 minutes or until cake springs back when lightly pressed. Cool in tin for 10 minutes before placing on a serving plate. Serve warm, drizzled with Chocolate Sauce and garnished with orange zest. To make the sauce, combine chocolate, cream and butter in a small saucepan. Stir over a low heat until chocolate and butter have melted and the sauce is smooth.

NOTE: As an alternative to the Chocolate Sauce, this cake is also delicious served with Raspberry Crème Fraîche Dip (see page 170).

CHOCOLATE FUDGE SELF-SAUCING PUDDING

SERVES 4

50 g butter
1½ cups Edmonds standard grade flour
2 teaspoons Edmonds baking powder
1 cup caster sugar
3 tablespoons cocoa
⅓ cup milk
2 teaspoons vanilla essence
¾ cup brown sugar
5 tablespoons cocoa
2 cups boiling water

Melt butter in a medium-sized microwave-proof pudding bowl. Stir in flour, baking powder, sugar, first measure of cocoa, milk and vanilla essence. Do not overbeat. Mix brown sugar and second measure of cocoa together. Sprinkle over mixture in bowl. Carefully pour the boiling water over. Cook in microwave, uncovered, on High (100%) for 12–14 minutes, until centre is just cooked. Allow to stand for 5 minutes before serving.

CHOCOLATE-GARNISHED HAZELNUT MERINGUE TORTE

8 egg whites
2 cups caster sugar
1 teaspoon white vinegar
1 teaspoon vanilla essence
1 tablespoon Edmonds Fielder's
   cornflour
½ cup roasted, shelled hazelnuts,
   finely chopped
2 tablespoons cocoa
whipped cream
whole hazelnuts and chocolate
   shavings to garnish

Preheat oven to 180°C. Draw three 20 cm round circles on baking paper. Lay baking paper on oven trays. Using an electric mixer, beat egg whites and caster sugar for 10–15 minutes or until thick and glossy. Mix vinegar, vanilla essence and cornflour to a smooth paste. Add to meringue. Beat on high speed for a further 3 minutes. Fold in hazelnuts and cocoa. Divide meringue evenly between the three circles, spreading to within 2 cm of the edge. Place meringue circles in oven. Turn oven temperature down to 100°C. Bake for 70 minutes. Turn off oven. Open oven door slightly and leave meringues in oven until cold. Carefully lift a meringue disc onto a serving plate. Smother with whipped cream, then top with another meringue disc. Cover with more whipped cream and top with remaining meringue disc. Cover top of torte with whipped cream. Garnish with whole hazelnuts and chocolate shavings.

COFFEE LIQUEUR CHEESECAKE

BASE
125 g plain sweet biscuits
¼ cup chopped walnuts
75 g butter, melted

FILLING
2 teaspoons instant coffee
¼ cup boiling water
3 tablespoons coffee liqueur
   (e.g. Tia Maria, Bailey's Irish Cream)
500 g cream cheese, softened
½ cup caster sugar
½ cup (125 g) sour cream
4 teaspoons gelatine
300 ml cream, lightly whipped

whipped cream, chocolate-coated
coffee beans or grated chocolate
to garnish

Place biscuits and walnuts in a food processor. Pulse until reduced to a coarse crumb. Add butter and pulse until combined. Press crumb mixture over the base of a greased 20 cm round springform tin that has the base lined with baking paper. Refrigerate while preparing the filling. In a small bowl, dissolve coffee in the boiling water. Stir in liqueur. Set aside to cool. Using an electric mixer, beat cream cheese and sugar until smooth. Add sour cream and beat until combined. Sprinkle gelatine over cooled coffee mixture. Sit the bowl over a bowl of hot water and stir until gelatine has dissolved. Using a large metal spoon, fold coffee mixture into cream cheese. Fold in whipped cream. Pour filling over prepared base. Cover and refrigerate for 6 hours. Decorate with whipped cream and chocolate-coated coffee beans or grated chocolate.

CRÉME BRÛLÉE

4 egg yolks
2 eggs
¼ cup caster sugar
½ teaspoon vanilla essence
1 cup cream
1 cup sugar

Beat egg yolks, eggs, caster sugar and vanilla essence together until combined. Mix in cream. Pour into four individual ½-cup ramekins and bake in a bain-marie (see page 230) at 160°C for 25 minutes or until brûlées are almost set. Alternatively, cook in a 3-cup capacity ovenproof dish. Remove from oven and leave to cool and firm. Sprinkle sugar over ramekins. Grill slowly until sugar is melted and golden. Serve immediately.

CRÉME CARAMEL

¾ cup sugar
½ cup water
2 cups milk
½ teaspoon vanilla essence
4 eggs
2 tablespoons sugar

Combine first measure of sugar and water in a heavy-based saucepan. Gently heat, stirring constantly until sugar has dissolved. Bring to the boil. Do not stir. Leave syrup to boil until golden. Divide syrup evenly among six individual ramekin dishes. Set aside. Heat milk until almost boiling. Remove from heat. Add vanilla essence. In a separate bowl, beat eggs and second measure of sugar together until pale. Pour heated milk onto egg mixture. Stir to combine. Strain. Divide egg mixture evenly among the caramel-lined dishes. Place dishes in a roasting dish. Pour in enough water to come halfway up the sides of ramekin dishes. Bake at 180°C for 35 minutes or until custard is set. Remove from roasting dish and allow to cool. Chill overnight then unmould onto serving plates.

COFFEE LIQUEUR CHEESECAKE ◈ 167

168 ◈ CRÉME BRÛLÉE

CRÉME CARAMEL ◈ 168

170 ◈ EASY CHOCOLATE MOUSSE

EASY CHOCOLATE MOUSSE

150 g cooking chocolate
4 eggs, separated
300 ml cream
2 tablespoons sugar
whipped cream
grated chocolate

Break chocolate into the top of a double boiler. Stir over hot water until chocolate has melted. Allow to cool slightly. Stir yolks into chocolate. Beat until thick and smooth. Beat cream until thick. Fold chocolate mixture into cream. Beat egg whites until stiff but not dry. Gradually add sugar, beating until thick and glossy. Fold half egg-white mixture into chocolate mixture until well mixed. Repeat with remaining egg-white mixture. Pour into four or six individual dishes or one large one. Chill until firm. Serve decorated with whipped cream and chocolate.

CHOCOLATE LIQUEUR MOUSSE
Add 1 tablespoon brandy, chocolate or coffee liqueur to melted chocolate.

FRESH SUMMER FRUIT PLATTER WITH RASPBERRY CRÈME FRAÎCHE DIP

1 cup fresh or frozen raspberries
1 tablespoon lemon juice
2 tablespoons icing sugar
300 g crème fraîche
selection of fresh summer fruit
   (e.g. peaches, apricots, nectarines, melon, strawberries, bananas, new season's apples)

To make the dip, place raspberries, lemon juice and icing sugar in a food processor. Pulse until raspberries are broken down. Transfer to a bowl and fold in crème fraîche. Refrigerate until required. To serve, place dip in a bowl in the centre of a platter. Surround with sliced fruit.

NOTE: Strawberries may be used as an alternative to raspberries for the dip. Cut strawberries in half before placing in food processor.

GINGERNUT CHEESECAKES

150 g Gingernut biscuits
500 g cream cheese
grated zest of 1 lemon
¼ cup lemon juice
¼ cup orange juice (1 orange)
½ cup caster sugar
lemon zest and fruit slices to serve

Put the biscuits into a plastic bag, seal and lightly crush with a rolling pin. Divide the crumbs between four parfait glasses. Put the cream cheese, lemon zest, lemon and orange juice and sugar in the large bowl of a food processor or mix with a wooden spoon until smooth. Spoon the mixture into the glasses and cover. Chill for 1 hour until the cream cheese has set. Garnish with lemon zest and slices of fruit.

GINGERNUT CHEESECAKES ▸ 170

173 ▸ LEMON TART

LEMON YOGHURT ICE CREAM TERRINE ▸ 175

175 ▸ MASCARPONE FLANS WITH PECAN PRALINE

ICE CREAM

4 eggs, separated
¼ cup caster sugar
¼ cup caster sugar
1 teaspoon vanilla essence
300 ml cream, whipped

VARIATIONS
1 cup chocolate chips
1 cup chopped nuts
1 cup puréed berry fruit
   (e.g. strawberries, raspberries)

Beat egg whites until stiff peaks form. Gradually add first measure of sugar, 1 tablespoon at a time, beating until sugar dissolves before adding the next tablespoon. In a separate bowl, beat egg yolks and second measure of sugar until thick and pale. Add vanilla essence. Gently fold yolk mixture into egg-white mixture. Fold cream into egg mixture. Add variations if desired. Pour mixture into a shallow container suitable for freezing. Freeze for 2 hours or until firm.

ICE CREAM TERRINE — CHOCOLATE AND APRICOT

CHOCOLATE ICE CREAM
100 g dark chocolate, chopped,
   or Melts
250 ml cream
3 eggs, separated
¼ cup caster sugar

APRICOT ICE CREAM
¾ cup dried apricots, roughly chopped
⅓ cup freshly squeezed orange juice
¼ cup brandy (or freshly squeezed
   orange juice)
3 eggs, separated
½ cup caster sugar
250 ml cream, whipped
chocolate curls and sliced apricots to
   garnish (optional)

To make the chocolate ice cream, place chocolate and a ¼ cup of the cream in a double boiler or heatproof bowl. Sit the bowl over a saucepan of simmering water. Stir continuously until the chocolate melts and the mixture is smooth. Cool slightly. Using an electric mixer, beat yolks and sugar until thick and pale. Add chocolate and beat until combined. Whip remaining cream. Fold cream into chocolate mixture. Beat egg whites until soft peaks form. Fold chocolate mixture into egg whites. Transfer to a 20 cm round springform tin, levelling the top with the back of a spoon. Cover and freeze for 4 hours.

To make the apricot ice cream, combine apricots and orange juice in a small saucepan. Stir over a medium heat until the juice is absorbed. Cool slightly. Place in a food processor with brandy and blend until smooth. Using an electric mixer, beat egg yolks and sugar until thick and pale. Beat in apricot purée. Beat egg whites until soft peaks form. Fold cream, then egg whites, into yolk mixture. Spoon over frozen chocolate ice cream. Cover and freeze for a further 4 hours. To serve, cut into wedges. Garnish with chocolate curls and sliced apricots.

INDIVIDUAL PAVLOVAS

4 egg whites
1½ cups caster sugar
1 teaspoon white vinegar
1 teaspoon vanilla essence
1 tablespoon Edmonds Fielder's
  cornflour
whipped cream
fresh berries and grated chocolate
  to garnish

Preheat oven to 180°C. Using an electric mixer, beat egg whites and caster sugar for 10–15 minutes or until thick and glossy. Mix vinegar, vanilla essence and cornflour together. Add to meringue. Beat on high speed for a further 5 minutes. Line a baking tray with baking paper. Draw four 12 cm round circles on the paper. Spread meringue to within 1 cm of the edge of the circles, keeping the shapes as round and even as possible. Place tray in preheated oven, then turn oven down to 100°C. Bake for 50 minutes. Turn off oven. Open door slightly and leave pavlovas until cold. Carefully lift pavlovas onto individual plates. Decorate with whipped cream, berries and grated chocolate.

LEMON TART

200 g Sweet Shortcrust Pastry
  (see page 224) or 200 g Edmonds
  sweet short pastry
4 egg yolks
¼ cup lemon juice
1 tablespoon grated lemon zest
½ cup caster sugar
1 cup full-cream milk

Roll pastry out on a lightly floured board to line a 20 cm pie or quiche dish. Bake blind (see page 230) at 200°C for 15 minutes. Remove baking-blind material and cook for a further 3 minutes. Beat egg yolks, lemon juice, lemon zest and sugar until combined. Lightly beat in milk. Pour into pastry shell. Bake at 200°C for 5 minutes, then reduce temperature to 150°C and cook for a further 20 minutes or until tart is set. Serve warm or cold.

LEMON YOGHURT ICE CREAM TERRINE

500 ml vanilla ice cream
500 g natural unsweetened yoghurt
¼ cup lemon curd
1 teaspoon grated lemon zest
lemon slices

Soften ice cream. Mix yoghurt, lemon curd and lemon zest together. Mix into softened ice cream. Line a 10 × 17 cm loaf tin with foil to cover base and long sides, not ends. Spoon mixture into prepared tin. Smooth surface. Cover with foil and freeze until firm. To serve, turn onto a serving plate. Garnish with lemon slices.

MASCARPONE FLANS WITH PECAN PRALINE

6 sheets Edmonds sweet short pastry

FILLING
2 teaspoons gelatine
1 tablespoon cold water
¼ cup liquid honey
1 teaspoon vanilla essence
250 g mascarpone
½ cup cream, whipped

PECAN PRALINE
½ cup sugar
½ cup pecan nuts

Using a 20 cm round guide, cut a circle from each sheet of pastry. Discard trimmings. Use pastry to line six 10 cm round loose-bottomed flan tins. Prick bases several times with a fork. Refrigerate for 15 minutes. Cover base of pastry cases with baking paper. Fill with dried beans, rice or other baking-blind material. Bake blind (see page 230) at 180°C for 12 minutes. Remove baking-blind material and bake for a further 8–10 minutes until golden. Cool. To make the filling, sprinkle gelatine over the cold water. Place over a bowl of hot water and stir until gelatine dissolves. Add honey and vanilla essence and beat into mascarpone with a wooden spoon. Fold in cream. Spoon filling into pastry shell, spreading evenly. Cover and refrigerate for at least 2 hours before serving. Just before serving, scatter Pecan Praline over flans.

To make the praline, place sugar in a small saucepan. Stir over a low heat until the sugar melts. Add pecan nuts. Increase heat slightly and, watching closely and stirring occasionally, allow the mixture to turn a light caramel colour. Spread mixture thinly on a greased baking tray. Allow to cool, then break into pieces. Either pulse to a coarse crumb in a food processor fitted with a metal blade or chop with a large sharp knife.

MOIST DATE PUDDING WITH BUTTERSCOTCH SAUCE ⟫ 177

177 ⟫ ORANGE-MARINATED STRAWBERRIES

PAVLOVA ROLL WITH APRICOT FILLING ⟫ 178

178 ⟫ PEAR AND GINGER UPSIDE-DOWN CAKE

MOIST DATE PUDDING WITH BUTTERSCOTCH SAUCE

1½ cups halved pitted dates
1½ cups water
1 teaspoon Edmonds baking soda
150 g butter, softened
1 cup brown sugar
⅓ cup golden syrup
2 eggs
1 teaspoon vanilla essence
2 cups Edmonds standard grade flour
1 teaspoon Edmonds baking powder
Butterscotch Sauce (see page 223)

Combine dates and water in a saucepan. Bring to the boil. Remove from heat and allow to cool to lukewarm. Stir in baking soda. Beat butter and sugar until light and creamy. Warm golden syrup slightly, then add to butter mixture. Beat well. Add eggs one at a time, beating well after each addition. Beat in vanilla essence. Sift flour and baking powder. Fold dry ingredients and date mixture alternately into butter mixture. Transfer to a greased 22 cm round cake tin lined with baking paper. Bake at 180°C for 50–55 minutes or until cake springs back when lightly pressed. Stand for 10 minutes before turning out and cutting into wedges. Serve warm, accompanied by Butterscotch Sauce.

ORANGE-MARINATED STRAWBERRIES

¼ cup thinly pared orange zest
1 cup orange juice
¼ cup sugar
1 large punnet or 400 g strawberries

Cut orange zest into thin strips. Place orange zest, juice and sugar in a saucepan. Bring to the boil and simmer for 5 minutes. Leave to cool. Hull strawberries and cut in half. Place in a bowl. Pour over orange mixture. Leave to marinate for 2 hours at room temperature or overnight in the refrigerator, mixing regularly. Serve lightly chilled.

PASSIONFRUIT FLAN

Sweet Shortcrust Pastry (see page 224) or 200 g Edmonds sweet short pastry

FILLING
4 eggs, lightly beaten
½ cup passionfruit pulp
¾ cup caster sugar
2 tablespoons Edmonds standard grade flour
¾ cup cream

whipped cream and passionfruit pulp to serve

Roll chilled pastry out on a lightly floured surface to fit a 24 cm round flan tin. Line tin with pastry. Cut off excess pastry. Freeze pastry case for 5 minutes. Bake blind (see page 230) at 190°C for 15 minutes. Remove baking-blind material and return to oven for 2–3 minutes to dry out the base. Turn down oven to 160°C. While pastry case is cooking, prepare the filling. Whisk all filling ingredients together in a bowl. Pour passionfruit filling into pastry case. Bake for 45–50 minutes or until filling is set. Serve at room temperature accompanied by whipped cream, drizzled with a little passionfruit pulp.

PAVLOVA ROLL WITH APRICOT FILLING

5 egg whites
1 cup caster sugar
1 teaspoon Edmonds Fielder's
   cornflour
1 teaspoon vanilla essence
1 teaspoon white vinegar
icing sugar to dust

APRICOT FILLING
400 g can apricots in light syrup
300 ml cream, lightly whipped

Using an electric mixer, beat egg whites and sugar for 10–15 minutes until thick and glossy. Mix cornflour to a paste with vanilla essence and vinegar. Add to meringue. Beat on high speed for a further 5 minutes. Thoroughly grease a 20 × 30 cm shallow baking tin. Line the base and sides with baking paper. Grease the baking paper. Preheat oven to 160°C. Spread meringue evenly over the base of the baking tin. Bake for 20 minutes until pale golden on top. The centre should be slightly soft. Remove from oven and stand for 5 minutes. Cut a piece of baking paper slightly longer than the baking tin. Lay on a flat surface. Dust thoroughly with icing sugar. Invert meringue onto the dusted paper. Peel off baking paper on the bottom of the meringue. Working quickly, roll meringue into a log, including the baking paper in the roll. Set aside to cool completely. To make the filling, drain apricots thoroughly. Place in a food processor and blend to a purée. Fold together whipped cream and apricot purée. Carefully unroll the meringue. Spread apricot filling evenly over the unrolled surface. Roll up into a log and serve immediately.

PEAR AND GINGER UPSIDE-DOWN PUDDING

3 tablespoons melted butter
½ cup brown sugar
2 tablespoons freshly squeezed
   orange juice
2 firm ripe pears, peeled, quartered
   and cored
whipped cream or ice cream to serve

BATTER
150 g butter, softened
1 cup brown sugar
2 eggs
2½ cups Edmonds standard grade flour
½ teaspoon Edmonds baking powder
3 teaspoons ground ginger
1 teaspoon Edmonds baking soda
1 cup warm milk

Grease the sides of a 23 cm round cake tin. Combine butter, brown sugar and orange juice. Mix well. Spread over the base of tin. Cut each pear quarter into four slices. Arrange in an overlapping pattern over the base of the baking tin. To make the batter, beat butter and brown sugar until light and creamy. Add eggs one at a time, beating well after each addition. Sift flour, baking powder and ginger. Dissolve baking soda in milk. Fold dry ingredients and milk alternately into butter mixture. Spoon over top of pears. Bake for 50–55 minutes or until a skewer inserted in centre of cake comes out clean. Stand for 5 minutes, then invert onto a serving plate. Serve warm with whipped cream or ice cream.

PEAR, APPLE AND GINGER
CRUMBLE WITH CUSTARD ◈ 181

PEAR, APPLE AND GINGER CRUMBLE WITH CUSTARD

3 apples, peeled, quartered, cored
  and sliced
3 pears, peeled, quartered, cored
  and sliced
¾ cup brown sugar
1 teaspoon cinnamon
1 tablespoon water
custard to serve

CRUMBLE
2 cups rolled oats
1 cup Edmonds standard grade flour
1 cup brown sugar
1½ teaspoons ground ginger
100 g butter, melted

Arrange fruit in a large ovenproof baking dish. Sprinkle sugar, cinnamon and water over. Combine crumble ingredients in a bowl. Mix well. Sprinkle crumble over fruit. Press lightly with the back of a spoon. Bake at 180°C for 45 minutes. Serve with custard.

PINEAPPLE AND GINGER STEAMED PUDDINGS

melted butter to grease
2 tablespoons golden syrup
1 tablespoon butter
440 g can pineapple rings in syrup,
  drained
100 g butter
⅓ cup golden syrup
⅓ cup sugar
1½ cups Edmonds standard grade flour
1 teaspoon Edmonds baking soda
1½ teaspoons ground ginger
1 egg, lightly beaten
¼ cup milk
custard or whipped cream to serve

Thoroughly grease six 9 cm round ramekins with melted butter. Place first measure of golden syrup and butter in a small saucepan. Stir over a low heat until butter has melted. Brush syrup over the base of the ramekins. Place a pineapple ring in the base of each ramekin. Combine second measure of butter, golden syrup and sugar in a saucepan. Stir over a low heat until butter has melted and mixture is smooth. Remove from heat. Sift together flour, baking soda and ginger. Make a well in the centre of dry ingredients. Pour in butter mixture. Beat lightly with a wooden spoon until ingredients are almost incorporated. Add egg and milk and mix well. Divide batter between the ramekins. Pour hot water into a roasting dish to a level of 3 cm. Sit ramekins in the water. Cover roasting dish tightly with foil. Bake at 180°C for 30 minutes or until a skewer inserted in the centre of a pudding comes out clean. Stand for 5 minutes before serving. To serve each pudding, run a knife around the inside of the ramekin. Place a serving plate over the ramekin and invert — the pudding should drop out. Serve with custard or cream.

QUICK APPLE AND BERRY CRUMBLE

2 × 567 g cans apple slices in natural
    juice
200 g blueberries (fresh or frozen)
¼ cup caster sugar

TOPPING
100 g butter
½ cup brown sugar
2½ cups rolled oats

Drain any juice from the apples. Spread apple evenly over the base of an ovenproof dish. Scatter berries over top. Sprinkle sugar over. To make the topping, place butter and brown sugar in a saucepan. Stir over a low heat until butter melts. Add rolled oats, mixing until thoroughly coated with butter mixture. Spoon crumble topping over fruit. Press down lightly with a fork. Bake at 180°C for 30 minutes until topping is golden and the fruit is beginning to bubble.

VARIATION
Add ½ cup chopped nuts or coconut to the topping mixture. Other berries can be used as an alternative to blueberries.

RICE PUDDING

5 tablespoons short-grain rice
2 tablespoons sugar
¾ cup sultanas (optional)
3 cups milk
2–3 drops vanilla essence
1 teaspoon butter
¼ teaspoon ground nutmeg
drained canned apricot halves to serve

Place rice, sugar and sultanas in the bottom of an ovenproof dish. Add milk and vanilla essence. Mix well. Add butter. Sprinkle nutmeg over surface. Cover and bake at 150°C for 2 hours, stirring two to three times in first hour. This pudding should be creamy when cooked. Serve with apricot halves.

SPICED PUMPKIN PIE ◈ 184

184 ◈ STEAMED CHOCOLATE PUDDINGS

SUMMER BERRIES WITH PRALINE AND CUSTARD ◈ 185

185 ◈ SUMMER PUDDING

SPICED PUMPKIN PIE

PASTRY

1¼ cups Edmonds standard grade flour
¼ cup icing sugar
100 g cold butter, chopped
1 egg yolk
1–2 tablespoons cold water

FILLING

500 g peeled, seeded crown pumpkin
¾ cup golden syrup
4 eggs, lightly beaten
½ cup cream
1 teaspoon cinnamon
¼ teaspoon ground nutmeg

whipped or clotted cream to serve

To make pastry, sift the flour and icing sugar into a bowl. Rub butter into the flour until mixture resembles coarse breadcrumbs. Add yolk and enough water to mix to a stiff dough. (Pastry can be made in a food processor.) Gather the dough into a ball, cover with plastic wrap and refrigerate for 30 minutes. To prepare the filling, chop pumpkin into chunks. Boil or microwave until tender. Drain well, then mash. While the pumpkin is still hot, stir in golden syrup. Mix well. Cool, then stir in remaining ingredients. Roll dough out on a lightly floured surface to fit a 24 cm round, 3.5 cm deep flan tin. Transfer dough to tin and trim off any excess. Prick the base. Refrigerate pastry base for 10 minutes, then freeze for 5 minutes. Bake blind (see page 230) at 190°C for 12 minutes. Remove baking-blind material and return to oven for 3–4 minutes to dry out pastry base. Reduce oven temperature to 180°C. Pour filling into pastry case. Bake for 45 minutes until filling has set. Serve warm with cream.

STEAMED CHOCOLATE PUDDINGS

2 cups Edmonds standard grade flour
1 teaspoon Edmonds baking powder
¼ cup cocoa
125 g butter, cut into cubes
100 g dark chocolate, chopped
¾ cup caster sugar
1 teaspoon vanilla essence
1 teaspoon Edmonds baking soda
1 cup milk, warmed
2 eggs, lightly beaten
butter for greasing
custard or cream to serve

Sift flour, baking powder and cocoa into a bowl. Combine butter, chocolate, sugar and vanilla essence in the top of a double boiler or in a heatproof bowl. Sit over simmering water. Stir constantly until butter and chocolate melt and mixture is smooth. Dissolve baking soda in milk. Fold butter mixture, milk and eggs into dry ingredients. Do not overmix. Thoroughly grease six ovenproof teacups or 1-cup-capacity ramekins with butter. Divide mixture evenly between prepared cups. Place cups in a roasting pan. Fill pan with hot water to halfway up the sides of the cups. Cover dish with a sheet of greaseproof paper, then a sheet of foil, securing the edges to seal in steam. Bake at 200°C for 45 minutes. Stand for 5 minutes before carefully removing the covers. Invert puddings onto warm serving plates. Serve with custard or cream.

SUMMER BERRIES WITH PRALINE AND CUSTARD

SERVES 4

2 tablespoons Edmonds custard
  powder
1 teaspoon sugar
1 cup milk
300 ml cream
3 cups mixed fresh berries
  (e.g. strawberries, raspberries,
  boysenberries and blueberries)

PRALINE
½ cup roasted almonds
  (see Nuts page 231)
½ cup sugar

Mix custard powder and sugar with ¼ cup of the measured milk in a saucepan. Stir in remaining milk. Heat to boiling then simmer for 2–3 minutes or until thickened. Stir constantly. Cover surface of custard with baking paper. Leave until cold. Whip cream until soft. Fold cream and custard together. Pile berries on a platter or in a bowl. Pour over custard mixture. Garnish with shards of praline.

PRALINE
Spread almonds on a baking tray. Gently heat sugar in a heavy frying pan until it starts to melt, and turn golden. Do not stir. Remove from heat. Pour over nuts on tray in a thin layer. Leave until hard and break into shards.

SUMMER PUDDING

SERVES 6–8

5 cups mixed berry fruit (washed,
  dried, hulled and sliced if large)
1¼ cups sugar
10 slices stale bread

Mix fruit and sugar together and heat gently until almost boiling. Remove from heat and cool. Cut crusts from bread and cut each slice into three fingers. Arrange bread around the inside of a 6-cup pudding basin. Spoon in one-third of the berry mixture. Layer with more bread then repeat, finishing with a layer of bread. Spoon over enough berry juice to moisten bread. Cover with plastic wrap and weigh down with a heavy weight. Refrigerate for 2 hours or overnight. Turn onto a serving plate and serve cut into wedges.

UPSIDE-DOWN PUDDING

SERVES 6

125 g butter
½ cup sugar
2 eggs
1 cup Edmonds standard grade flour
2 teaspoons Edmonds baking powder
2 tablespoons milk
25 g butter, melted
¼ cup brown sugar
1 teaspoon mixed spice
2 × 425 g cans pear halves, drained

Cream first measure of butter and sugar until light and fluffy. Add eggs one at a time, beating well after each addition. Sift flour and baking powder together. Fold into creamed mixture. Stir in milk. Combine second measure of butter, sugar and mixed spice. Spread this mixture onto the base of a 20 cm round cake tin. Arrange pears, cut-side down, on the butter mixture. Spoon cake mixture over fruit. Bake at 180°C for 40 minutes or until cake springs back when lightly touched. Unmould onto a serving plate.

WARM GINGERBREAD DATE CAKE

1 cup pitted dates, roughly chopped
1½ cups water
¾ teaspoon Edmonds baking soda
2 eggs
¾ cup brown sugar
½ cup canola oil
¼ cup golden syrup
¼ cup chopped crystallised ginger
2½ cups Edmonds standard grade flour
2 tablespoons cocoa
1 teaspoon Edmonds baking powder
2 teaspoons ground ginger
icing sugar to dust
whipped cream to serve

Combine dates and water in a small saucepan. Bring to the boil. Remove from heat and stir in baking soda. Cool for 10 minutes. In a large bowl, whisk together eggs, sugar, oil, golden syrup and crystallised ginger. Sift together flour, cocoa, baking powder and ground ginger. Stir date mixture into egg mixture. Lastly, fold in dry ingredients. Spoon into a greased 22 cm round cake tin that has been lined with baking paper. Bake at 180°C for 50–55 minutes or until a skewer inserted in the centre of the cake comes out clean. Stand for 10 minutes before turning onto a wire rack. Serve warm or cold, dusted with icing sugar and accompanied by cream.

ZUCCOTTO

SERVES 8

400 g Ernest Adams unfilled sponge
½ cup Cointreau or Maraschino or
   Grand Marnier to brush
500 ml cream, lightly whipped
100 g dark chocolate, or chocolate
   buttons, melted and cooled slightly
½ cup chocolate chips
¼ cup finely chopped red glacé cherries
¼ cup finely chopped glacé pineapple
⅓ cup chopped, roasted, shelled
   hazelnuts
cocoa to dust

Line a 6-cup-capacity basin with plastic wrap so it extends over sides of basin. Cut sponge into 1.5 cm wide strips, tapering them at the ends, so they are long enough to line the basin. Brush sponge strips with liqueur. Line basin with sponge, reserving some for top of pudding. Brush sponge lining the basin with more liqueur to completely soak. Divide cream equally between two bowls. Fold one portion into the melted chocolate, one tablespoon at a time. Cover sponge with chocolate mixture, leaving a cavity. Cover and refrigerate for 2 hours. Fold chocolate chips, cherries, pineapple and hazelnuts into remaining cream. Spoon into cavity. Brush remaining sponge strips with liqueur and arrange over filling to cover. Cover with plastic wrap that is overhanging the basin. Weight with a heavy object. Refrigerate for 8 hours or overnight. To remove from basin, unfold plastic wrap and place a serving dish over the bowl. Carefully invert bowl to release pudding. Remove plastic wrap. Dust with sifted cocoa.

UPSIDE-DOWN PUDDING **185**

186 WARM GINGERBREAD DATE CAKE

ZUCCOTTO **186**

188 CHEESEBOARD

CHEESEBOARDS

A cheeseboard makes a wonderful alternative to dessert. Cheeseboards can also be served before the dessert course, as the French do. Simplicity is the key to a well-presented cheeseboard. The following guidelines will assist in achieving a superb result:

Offer two or three reasonable-sized pieces of cheese rather than numerous small ones that will dry out quickly and look unappetising.

Select different types of cheese from the categories listed below, for an interesting presentation.

To ensure the cheeseboard is visually attractive, use different shaped cheeses, for example, a wedge, a log and a cylinder of cheese.

Remove cheese from the refrigerator at least 1 hour before serving. This allows the cheese to come back to room temperature where the flavour is best appreciated.

Keep garnishes simple — slices of crisp apple, a handful of quality shelled walnuts or a small bunch of grapes is all that is required.

Serve unsalted crackers or sliced French or walnut bread with the cheeseboard. Place them on a separate plate. (If placed directly alongside cheese, crackers can absorb moisture and become soft.)

CHEESE CATEGORIES

FRESH CHEESE Fresh cheeses have a high moisture content and therefore a relatively short shelf life. They do not have a rind. Fresh cheeses include ricotta, fresh mozzarella, cream cheese, cottage cheese and feta.

SOFT WHITE CHEESE Covered with a white rind, soft white cheeses begin ripening from the outside. If the interior of the cheese is chalky in appearance, it is not completely ripe. When at its prime for eating, the interior should be creamy and soft. Examples include camembert and brie.

SEMI-SOFT CHEESE A springy texture is characteristic of semi-soft cheeses. They are often covered with a wax rind and are suited to use in cooking. Edam, gouda and raclette are semi-soft cheeses.

HARD CHEESE Hard cheeses mature slowly. The most common example is cheddar. Parmesan and gruyere also fall into this category. The texture of hard cheeses varies widely.

BLUE CHEESE Blue mould is added to the milk, then metal rods are used to pierce the cheese, allowing air to enter and thus encouraging the mould to grow.

SPECIALTY CHEESES This category includes any cheeses that have ingredients such as nuts, herbs or fruit flavourings.

SPECIAL OCCASIONS

HOT ORANGE-GLAZED HAM ON THE BONE » 191

192 « MEDLEY OF SUMMER VEGETABLES

MINI SAUSAGES WITH BACON » 192

192 « MINTED BABY POTATOES

CHRISTMAS IDEAS

AÏOLI

MAKES 1 CUP

2 egg yolks
1 teaspoon crushed garlic
1 tablespoon lemon juice
1 cup extra virgin olive oil
salt and freshly ground black pepper
   to season

Place egg yolks, garlic and lemon juice in a food processor. Blend until smooth. With the motor running, gradually add oil, a little at a time. The mixture will thicken. (If the oil is added too quickly, the Aïoli will curdle.) Season to taste. Serve, chilled, with Medley of Summer Vegetables (see page 192).

NOTE: The aïoli may become very thick when refrigerated. For a more manageable consistency, add a little more lemon juice before serving.

HOT ORANGE-GLAZED HAM ON THE BONE

SERVES 6

cooked ham on the bone
whole cloves
½ cup orange marmalade
juice of 1 orange
¼ cup brown sugar
2 tablespoons sherry

Remove rind from ham by cutting through the skin at the shank end with a small knife. Make an incision lengthwise down the middle of the rind, starting from the shank-end cut. Insert thumb under the incision and ease rind off one half of ham. Repeat with other side. Trim off any excess fat. Using a small sharp knife, score fat on the diagonal to a depth of 2 mm, then crossways to make diamonds. Push a clove into the centre of each diamond. Cover shank end with foil. Place ham on a rack in a large roasting dish. Combine marmalade, orange juice, brown sugar and sherry in a small saucepan. Stir over a medium heat until sugar has dissolved and glaze comes to the boil. Reduce heat and simmer for 5 minutes, stirring occasionally. Spoon half the glaze thickly over the ham, covering exposed fat. Bake at 160°C, allowing 10 minutes per 500 g. Baste 3–4 times during the cooking with remaining glaze. Set aside for 10 minutes before carving.

NOTE: To store leftover ham, cover with a clean damp teatowel and refrigerate. Change the teatowel daily.

MEDLEY OF SUMMER VEGETABLES

4 capsicums, any colour
6 small courgettes
6 scallopini (optional)
18 asparagus spears
100 g green beans
3 tablespoons extra virgin olive oil
rock salt or sea salt to sprinkle
Aïoli (see page 191)

Prepare vegetables. Cut capsicums in half, remove core and seeds, then cut in half again. Trim ends from courgettes, then cut in half lengthwise. Cut scallopini in half. Snap woody ends off asparagus. Trim beans. Preheat oven to 220°C. Pour oil into a roasting dish. Heat dish in oven for 5 minutes. Add vegetables and toss to coat with oil. Sprinkle with salt. Return pan to oven. Cook vegetables until just tender, turning frequently. The vegetables will cook at different rates — transfer to a warm dish when done. Serve accompanied by Aïoli.

MINI SAUSAGES WITH BACON

24 mini sausages or saveloys
12 rashers streaky bacon

Cut the rashers of bacon in half, widthways. Wrap each sausage in a piece of bacon, tucking the ends underneath. Place the sausages in a roasting tray and bake in oven at 180°C for 15 minutes, until bacon is crispy and sausages are cooked. Serve arranged around the Christmas turkey.

NOTE: Spicy sausages such as small chorizo are also perfect for this recipe.

MINTED BABY POTATOES

new baby potatoes, scrubbed
3–4 sprigs of mint
knob of butter

Cook potatoes with the mint in boiling water until they are tender. Drain. Remove mint. Add butter and toss lightly until butter melts and potatoes are evenly coated.

PAWPAW AND CORIANDER SALSA

½ pawpaw, seeded and peeled
2 spring onions, finely chopped
2 tablespoons chopped coriander
1 tablespoon lemon juice
freshly ground black pepper to season

Chop pawpaw into small cubes. Put all ingredients into a glass or ceramic bowl. Stir gently to combine. Cover and refrigerate for at least 30 minutes before serving. This salsa can be made up to 1 day before required.

ROAST CHICKEN WITH WILD RICE AND CASHEW NUT STUFFING

STUFFING

½ cup wild rice
1 tablespoon canola oil
1 onion, finely chopped
1 teaspoon crushed garlic
100 g button mushrooms, sliced
½ cup fresh breadcrumbs
½ cup (70 g) roughly chopped roasted
  cashew nuts
1 egg
salt and freshly ground black pepper
  to season

1 × no. 18 chicken
gravy to serve

To make the stuffing, cook rice in boiling water, or microwave until tender. Tip into a sieve. Refresh under cold running water. Drain thoroughly. While the rice is cooking, heat oil in a frying pan. Cook onion for 5 minutes until soft. Add garlic and mushrooms and cook for 6–8 minutes until pan is dry. Combine all stuffing ingredients in a bowl. Mix well. Remove giblets from chicken. (If desired use to make gravy or stock.) Rinse out cavity with cold running water. Drain. Pat chicken dry with paper towels. Spoon stuffing into cavity. Close the cavity using a wooden skewer. Cross legs of chicken and tie with string, including the parson's nose, so the legs are neatly placed over the chicken. Bake at 180°C for 2 hours or until juices run clear. Remove from oven and stand for 5–10 minutes in a warm place before carving. Serve with gravy.

VEGETABLES

ROAST VEGETABLES

To prepare for roasting, peel vegetables such as potatoes, kumara and parsnip. Seed pumpkin. Cut vegetables into chunks. One hour before the chicken is cooked, add vegetables to the roasting pan, turning to coat with pan juices. For a golden-brown finish to the vegetables, turn oven to grill for 3–4 minutes once the chicken has been removed.

STEAMED VEGETABLES

Choose a selection of the following seasonal vegetables to accompany the roast vegetables: carrots, beans, asparagus, broccoli, brussels sprouts. Bring a little water to the boil in a saucepan and steam vegetables until just tender. Drain.

ROAST TURKEY

4.5–5.5 kg turkey (thawed if it was frozen)
50 g butter, at room temperature
sage and parsley sprigs to garnish

STUFFING
1 onion, finely chopped
8 rashers streaky bacon, diced
250 g fresh white breadcrumbs
350 g sausage meat
2 tablespoons mixed herbs
juice of 1 lemon
2 eggs

Preheat oven to 190°C. Remove giblets from turkey and wash the bird inside and out. Dry well with kitchen paper. To prepare stuffing, sauté onions and bacon together for 5 minutes until onion is softened. Mix bacon and onion with all remaining ingredients in a large bowl. Spoon stuffing into cavity. Close cavity using a wooden skewer. Cross legs of turkey and tie together with string. Grease a large roasting pan with butter. Smear the rest over the turkey skin and season well, then put in the pan. Loosely cover with foil and roast. A turkey should be roasted at 18 minutes per 450 g plus 25 minutes finishing time. Baste every hour. One hour before the end of cooking, remove foil and drain off excess fat. To test whether turkey is cooked, insert a skewer into thickest part of thigh — the juices should run clear. If they are pinkish, cook for 15 minutes more, then test again. Serve on a large platter garnished with vegetables, stuffing, sage and parsley.

CHRISTMAS CAKE

1¾ cups orange juice
¾ cup dark rum or brandy
2 tablespoons grated orange zest
500 g currants
500 g raisins
2 cups sultanas
2 cups chopped dates
150 g crystallised ginger, chopped
150 g packet mixed peel
150 g packet glacé cherries, halved
½ teaspoon vanilla essence
¼ teaspoon almond essence
2 teaspoons grated lemon zest
1 cup blanched almonds
2½ cups Edmonds high grade flour
½ teaspoon Edmonds baking soda
1 teaspoon cinnamon
1 teaspoon mixed spice
½ teaspoon ground nutmeg
250 g butter, softened
1½ cups brown sugar
2 tablespoons treacle
5 eggs

In a saucepan, bring to the boil orange juice, rum and orange zest. Remove from heat and add dried fruit. Cover and leave fruit to soak overnight. Stir vanilla and almond essences, lemon zest and almonds into saucepan. Sift flour, soda and spices into a bowl. In a separate large bowl, cream butter, sugar and treacle until light and fluffy. Add eggs one at a time, beating well after each addition. Into this mixture, fold sifted ingredients alternately with fruit mixture. Line a deep, square 23 cm tin with two layers of brown paper followed by one layer of baking paper. Spoon mixture into tin. Bake at 150°C for 4 hours or until an inserted skewer comes out clean when tested. Leave in tin until cold. Wrap in foil. Store in a cool place. Ice if wished.

CHRISTMAS COOKIES

125 g butter, softened
¾ cup caster sugar
1 egg
1 teaspoon vanilla essence
2 cups Edmonds standard grade flour
½ teaspoon Edmonds baking powder
¼ cup cocoa
narrow ribbon to hang biscuits

Cream butter and sugar until light and fluffy. Add egg. Beat well. Beat in vanilla essence. Sift flour, baking powder and cocoa. Stir into creamed mixture, mixing to a soft dough. Shape dough into a ball. Cover with plastic wrap and refrigerate for 30 minutes. Roll dough out on a floured surface to a thickness of 5 mm. Using Christmas-shaped biscuit cutters, stamp out shapes. Place on greased oven trays. Using a metal or wooden skewer, make a small hole in the top of each biscuit. Bake at 180°C for 12 minutes. Cool on wire racks. To hang the biscuits from the Christmas tree, thread ribbon through the hole in the top of each biscuit, tying the ends together.

CHRISTMAS MINCEMEAT

MAKES 6 CUPS

2 medium apples, unpeeled, quartered
  and cored
100 g suet
1¼ cups currants
1¼ cups sultanas
1¼ cups raisins
1¼ cups mixed peel
¼ cup blanched almonds
1 cup brown sugar
¼ teaspoon salt
½ teaspoon ground nutmeg
2 tablespoons brandy or whisky or
  lemon juice

Mince or finely chop apples, suet, currants, sultanas, raisins, peel and almonds. Add sugar, salt, nutmeg and brandy. Mix well. Spoon mixture into clean jars and seal. If using lemon juice, refrigerate.

LIGHT CHRISTMAS MINCEMEAT
Omit suet and store mincemeat in refrigerator.

CHRISTMAS MINCE PIES

MAKES 16

400 g Sweet Shortcrust Pastry
  (see page 224) or 400 g Edmonds
  sweet short pastry
1 cup Christmas Mincemeat
1 egg, beaten
icing sugar

On a lightly floured board, roll out pastry to 3 mm thickness. Cut out rounds using a 7 cm cutter, and use to line about 16 patty tins. Using a 6 cm round cutter, cut out tops from remaining pastry. Spoon teaspoons of mincemeat into each base. Brush edges of bases with some of the egg. Place tops over filling, pressing slightly around edges to seal the pies. Glaze with remaining beaten egg. Bake at 180°C for 15 minutes or until lightly browned. To serve, heat at 140°C for 15 minutes or until warm. Dust with sifted icing sugar.

CHRISTMAS PUDDING ⟫ 198

198 ⟫ HAZELNUT CHOCOLATE TRUFFLES

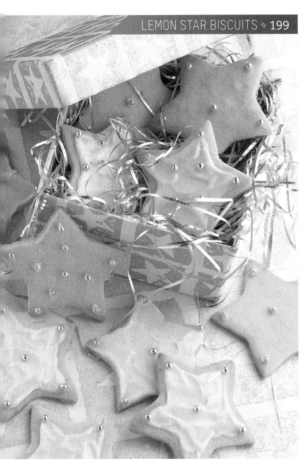

LEMON STAR BISCUITS ⟫ 199

199 ⟫ PANETTONE

CHRISTMAS PUDDING

1 cup sultanas
1 cup raisins
1 cup currants
70 g packet blanched almonds, chopped
150 g packet mixed peel
1 cup shredded suet
1 cup Edmonds standard grade flour
1½ teaspoons Edmonds baking powder
1 teaspoon mixed spice
1 teaspoon cinnamon
¼ teaspoon ground nutmeg
¼ teaspoon salt
1½ cups soft breadcrumbs
1 cup brown sugar
2 eggs
2 teaspoons grated lemon zest
½ cup milk
1 tablespoon brandy

Put sultanas, raisins, currants, almonds and mixed peel into a large bowl. Add suet, mixing to combine. Sift flour, baking powder, mixed spice, cinnamon, nutmeg and salt into fruit mixture. Mix well. Add breadcrumbs and mix through. In a separate bowl, beat brown sugar, eggs, lemon zest and milk together. Add to fruit mixture, mixing thoroughly to combine. Stir in brandy. Spoon mixture into a well-greased 6-cup-capacity pudding basin. Cover with pleated greaseproof paper or foil. Secure with string, leaving a loop to lift out pudding when cooked. Place a trivet or old saucer in the bottom of a large saucepan half filled with boiling water. Carefully lower pudding into saucepan, making sure the water comes two-thirds of the way up the sides of basin. Cover and cook for 5 hours, making sure water is constantly bubbling. Check water level from time to time. Remove from saucepan. Leave until cold. Wrap well and store in refrigerator until ready to use. Steam for a further 2 hours before serving. Serve with custard.

HAZELNUT CHOCOLATE TRUFFLES

250 g dark chocolate, chopped
25 g butter, chopped
½ cup cream
1 tablespoon Frangelico liqueur (optional)
¼ cup ground roasted hazelnuts
200 g dark chocolate, chopped
21 hazelnuts, halved, to garnish

Place chocolate and butter in the top of a double boiler or a heatproof bowl. Place over simmering water. Stir constantly until chocolate melts and the mixture is smooth. Remove from heat. Stir in cream, liqueur and ground hazelnuts. Cover and refrigerate for several hours until firm. Roll teaspoons of mixture into balls. Place in a single layer on a plate. Cover with plastic wrap and refrigerate for 1 hour. To coat truffles, melt second measure of chocolate as above. Cool slightly. Quickly dip truffles into the melted chocolate, using a dipping stick or teaspoons. Allow excess chocolate to drain off. Place on a sheet of foil. Garnish each truffle with half a hazelnut. Allow to dry before storing in a covered container in a cool place.

LEMON STAR BISCUITS

125 g butter, softened
¾ cup caster sugar
1 egg
2 teaspoons finely grated lemon zest
2 cups Edmonds standard grade flour

LEMON ICING
1 cup icing sugar
2 teaspoons butter, softened
1 tablespoon lemon juice
boiling water to mix
silver balls to decorate (optional)

Cream butter and caster sugar until light and fluffy. Add egg and lemon zest. Beat well. Sift flour. Stir into creamed mixture, mixing to a soft dough. Shape dough into a ball. Cover with plastic wrap and refrigerate for 30 minutes. Roll dough out on a floured surface to a thickness of 5 mm. Using a star-shaped biscuit cutter, stamp out shapes. Place on greased oven trays. Bake at 180°C for 12 minutes until lightly golden. Cool on wire racks. To make icing, sift icing sugar into a bowl. Mix in butter and lemon juice. Add just enough water to achieve a spreadable consistency. When biscuits are cold, spread with Lemon Icing and decorate with silver balls.

PANETTONE

1 teaspoon sugar
¼ cup warm water
4 teaspoons Edmonds active yeast
¾ cup milk
75 g butter
4 cups Edmonds high grade flour
⅓ cup sugar
½ teaspoon salt
4 egg yolks, lightly beaten
¾ cup sultanas
¼ cup mixed peel
finely grated zest of 1 lemon
milk to brush

NOTE: Panettone is best eaten on the day it is made. However, it will keep for up to 4 days. It is delicious toasted.

Dissolve first measure of sugar in warm water. Sprinkle yeast over water. Set aside in a warm place for 10 minutes until frothy. Place milk and butter in a small saucepan. Stir over a low heat until butter melts. Transfer to a large bowl and allow to cool to lukewarm. Stir in frothy yeast mixture. Using a wooden spoon, beat in 1 cup of the flour, and the sugar and salt. Cover with plastic wrap. Stand in a warm place until mixture is bubbly. Mix yolks and remaining flour into yeast mixture. Add sultanas, mixed peel and lemon zest. Mix to a soft dough with a wooden spoon. Turn dough onto a floured surface. Knead for 10 minutes until smooth and elastic. Place dough in a lightly oiled bowl, turning to coat with oil. Cover with plastic wrap. Stand in a warm place until doubled in bulk (about 1½ hours). Punch dough down with a fist, then knead for 1 minute on a lightly floured surface. Form into a large ball and place in a greased, deep, 20 cm round cake tin that has the base lined with baking paper. Cover with plastic wrap. Stand in a warm place until doubled in bulk. Brush top of risen dough with milk. Bake in lower third of the oven at 200°C for 15 minutes, then reduce to 180°C and bake for a further 30 minutes or until bread sounds hollow when tapped. Leave in tin for 10 minutes before transferring to a wire rack to cool. Serve buttered.

PANFORTE

1 cup hazelnuts, toasted and roughly
   chopped
1 cup blanched almonds, toasted and
   roughly chopped
½ cup dried figs, chopped
½ cup dried apricots, chopped
¼ cup crystallised ginger, chopped
¼ cup mixed peel
¾ cup Edmonds high grade flour
1 teaspoon cinnamon
¾ teaspoon ground nutmeg
¼ teaspoon ground cloves
½ cup liquid honey
½ cup caster sugar

Thoroughly grease a 20 cm round cake tin. Line the base and sides with baking paper. Combine nuts, dried fruit, flour and spices in a mixing bowl. Mix well. Place honey and sugar in a small saucepan. Stir over a low heat until sugar dissolves. Bring to the boil, stirring constantly. Boil for about 2 minutes until mixture reaches the soft-ball stage. (To test for soft-ball stage, drop a small amount of mixture off a teaspoon into cold water. When a soft ball forms, the mixture is ready. On a sugar thermometer, the soft-ball stage is 116°C.) Do not let the syrup change colour. Remove from the heat and let the bubbles subside. Carefully pour syrup over dry ingredients, then quickly mix to combine. Press into prepared tin. (Speed is vital, as the mixture will become sticky and unmanageable very quickly.) Bake at 150°C for 45 minutes in the lower third of the oven. Cool in tin. Wrap in foil and store in the refrigerator. To serve, cut into thin wedges.

PAVLOVA

SERVES 6

4 egg whites
1½ cups caster sugar
1 teaspoon white vinegar
1 teaspoon vanilla essence
1 tablespoon Edmonds Fielder's
   cornflour
whipped cream
fresh berries and mint leaves
   to garnish

Preheat oven to 180°C. Using an electric mixer, beat egg whites and caster sugar for 10–15 minutes or until thick and glossy. Mix vinegar, vanilla essence and cornflour together. Add to meringue. Beat on high speed for a further 5 minutes. Line an oven tray with baking paper. Draw a 22 cm circle on the baking paper. Spread the pavlova to within 2 cm of the edge of the circle, keeping the shape as round and even as possible. Smooth top surface. Place pavlova in preheated oven then turn oven tenperature down to 100°C. Bake pavlova for 1 hour. Turn off oven. Open oven door slightly and leave pavlova in oven until cold. Place on a serving plate. Decorate with whipped cream, fresh berries and mint leaves.

STAINED-GLASS-WINDOW LOG

¾ cup Brazil nuts, toasted and roughly
  chopped
10 red glacé cherries, halved
10 green glacé cherries, halved
12 dried apricots, quartered
250 g dark chocolate, roughly chopped
½ cup sweetened condensed milk
3 tablespoons cream

Combine nuts and dried fruit in a bowl. Place chocolate, condensed milk and cream in the top of a double boiler or heatproof bowl. Place over simmering water. Stir constantly until chocolate melts and mixture is smooth. Remove from heat. Add nut and fruit mixture. Mix well. Lay a 45 cm length of foil on a flat surface. Transfer chocolate mixture to the centre of the foil. Fold the foil over the mixture, then roll into a log about 35 cm long. Twist the ends of the foil to enclose the log. Refrigerate for 3–4 hours until firm. To serve, cut into slices. Store in the refrigerator.

TIRAMISU TERRINE

SERVES 6–8

3 teaspoons instant coffee
¾ cup boiling water
¼ cup brandy
250 g packet sponge fingers (savoiardi
  biscuits)
100 g dark chocolate, chopped
300 ml cream
1 teaspoon gelatine
1 tablespoon cold water
¼ cup icing sugar
300 g mascarpone cheese
10–12 whole strawberries, hulled

Dissolve coffee in boiling water. Stir in brandy. Line an 11 × 21 cm loaf tin with plastic wrap so that it extends over the sides of the tin. One by one, quickly dip eight biscuits into the coffee mixture. Line the base of the tin with the biscuits. Keep remaining coffee mixture. Combine chocolate and ¼ cup of the cream in the top of a double boiler or heatproof bowl. Place over simmering water. Stir constantly until chocolate melts and the mixture is smooth. Remove from heat. Sprinkle gelatine over cold water. Place over a bowl of hot water and stir until gelatine dissolves. Stir into chocolate. Whip remaining cream and icing sugar together. Place mascarpone in a medium bowl. Beat with a wooden spoon until smooth. Fold in cream and chocolate. Spoon half the mixture evenly over biscuits. Place the strawberries in a line down the middle of the chocolate mixture. Carefully spoon over remaining chocolate mixture. Dip eight more biscuits in reserved coffee mixture. Arrange on top of chocolate layer to cover completely. Fold plastic wrap over the terrine. Refrigerate for 4 hours. To serve, unfold plastic wrap from the top of the terrine. Invert onto a board or flat surface. Using a sharp knife, cut into slices.

CELEBRATION MENU

Whether for a mid-winter dinner or a birthday celebration, the following menu is guaranteed to be a winner!

1 CREAMY TOMATO AND BASIL SOUP *(see page 204)*

2 ROASTED ROOT VEGETABLES *(see page 205)*

3 ROAST PORK LOIN WITH LEEK AND PISTACHIO STUFFING *(see page 204)*

3 GINGER SESAME BEANS *(see page 205)*

4 RUSTIC RHUBARB AND APPLE TARTS *(see page 205)*

PREPARE AHEAD
1 Make the soup the day before.
2 Make the stuffing for the pork loin the day before.

ON THE DAY
1 Stuff pork loin and cook.
2 Prepare and cook vegetables.
3 Prepare tarts.
4 Refrigerate and cook tarts as the main course is served.

CREAMY TOMATO AND BASIL SOUP

SERVES 4

1 tablespoon pure olive oil
1 onion, finely chopped
1 teaspoon crushed garlic
2 × 400 g cans tomatoes in juice,
    chopped
1 tablespoon sugar
375 ml chicken or vegetable stock
½ cup light cream
2 tablespoons shredded basil leaves
salt and freshly ground black pepper
    to season
shredded basil leaves to garnish

Heat oil in a large, heavy-based saucepan. Cook onion for 4–5 minutes until soft. Add garlic, tomatoes, sugar and stock. Bring to the boil. Reduce heat and simmer for 20 minutes. Purée in batches in a food processor. Return to saucepan. Add cream and basil. Heat gently — do not allow to boil. Season to taste. Ladle into warm bowls. Garnish with basil.

ROAST PORK LOIN WITH LEEK AND PISTACHIO STUFFING

SERVES 8

STUFFING
2 tablespoons pure olive oil
1 small leek, thinly sliced and washed
1 cup fresh breadcrumbs
1 small apple, grated
⅓ cup pistachio nuts
1 tablespoon chopped marjoram
salt and freshly ground black pepper
    to season

2 kg boneless loin of pork
pure olive oil to coat
sea or rock salt to rub
gravy to serve

To make the stuffing, heat oil in a heavy-based frying pan. Cook leeks for 8–10 minutes until soft and all liquid has evaporated. Combine all stuffing ingredients in a bowl. Mix well. Preheat oven to 250°C. Lay pork loin skin-side up on a flat surface. Using a sharp knife, score at 1.5 cm intervals through the skin and just into the layer of fat beneath the skin. Turn loin over. Spread stuffing along the fillet at one end. Roll up and secure at regular intervals with string. Rub skin with oil and salt. Bake for 20 minutes until the skin is blistered and golden — crackling has formed. Reduce temperature to 160°C and cook for a further 1½–2 hours. Stand for 15 minutes before removing string and carving. Serve with gravy.

NOTE: As a general guide, pork takes an hour per kilogram to roast at 160–170°C, including the time for forming the crackling. A meat thermometer is the best way to ensure that the meat is cooked — insert into the thickest part of the meat. At 71°C the meat is medium done and at 76°C it is well done.

GINGER SESAME BEANS

2 teaspoons sesame oil
300 g green beans, ends trimmed
2 teaspoons finely grated root ginger
2 tablespoons toasted sesame seeds

Heat oil in a heavy-based frying pan or wok. Stir-fry beans and ginger for 3–4 minutes until tender. Sprinkle over sesame seeds, tossing to coat.

ROASTED ROOT VEGETABLES

selection of root vegetables
    (e.g. potatoes, kumara, pumpkin,
    carrots, parsnips)
extra virgin olive oil
rock salt (or regular salt) to sprinkle

Scrub or peel vegetables, as desired, then cut into chunks or lengths of approximately the same size. Preheat oven to 200°C. Pour a little oil over the base of a roasting dish. Heat dish in oven for 2–3 minutes. Add vegetables and toss to combine. Sprinkle over a little salt. Roast for 15–30 minutes (depending on the size of the vegetable chunks) until vegetables are tender and golden. If the vegetables are tender, but not as golden as you would like, turn oven to grill and cook vegetables to the desired colour.

RUSTIC RHUBARB AND APPLE TARTS

2 medium Granny Smith apples
250 g (3 stalks) rhubarb, washed
½ cup brown sugar
2 tablespoons Edmonds standard
    grade flour
2 teaspoons grated lemon zest
4 sheets Edmonds sweet short pastry
lemon zest to garnish (optional)
whipped cream to serve

Peel, core and quarter apples. Cut into 1.5 cm chunks. Cut rhubarb into 1.5 cm lengths. Combine fruit, sugar, flour and zest in a bowl. Mix well. Using a 20 cm round guide, cut a circle from each sheet of pastry. Discard trimmings. Pile one quarter of the fruit mixture onto the pastry, leaving a 4 cm border. Working around the filling, gather up the pastry, pleating it in one direction and folding the pastry onto itself in regularly spaced pleats. Transfer to a baking tray. Repeat with remaining pastry and fruit, to give four tarts. Refrigerate for 15 minutes. Bake at 180°C for 30 minutes or until fruit is tender and pastry is golden. Stand for 10 minutes before serving. Garnish with lemon zest. Serve with whipped cream.

NOTE: This recipe makes four large individual tarts. For a more modest serving, halve the recipe to make two tarts and cut in half to serve.

MENU IDEAS

VEGETARIAN DINNER PARTY

SPRING ROLLS WITH CHILLI DIPPING SAUCE (see page 94)

VEGETABLE, CASHEW NUT AND HOKKIEN NOODLE STIR-FRY (see page 109)

MOIST DATE PUDDING WITH BUTTERSCOTCH SAUCE (see page 177)

ALFRESCO LUNCH

GUACAMOLE (see page 86) Serve with corn chips or CROSTINI (see page 84)

CHICKEN CAESAR SALAD (see page 70) (serve with fresh crusty bread)

ORANGE POLENTA CAKE (see page 18)

WEEKEND BREAKFAST

CHUNKY HONEY TOASTED MUESLI (see page 66)

EGGS BENEDICT (see page 68)

BLUEBERRY CREAM CHEESE LOAF (see page 59)

FINGER FOOD FOR TEENAGERS GET-TOGETHER

GUACAMOLE (see page 86) (serve with corn chips)

SPICY CAJUN POTATO WEDGES (see page 94)

SESAME-MARINATED CHICKEN NIBBLES (see page 92)

WHITE AND DARK CHOCOLATE BROWNIE SLICE (see page 52)

MINI PECAN TARTLETS (see page 63)

NO-FUSS MID-WEEK DINNER PARTY

ANTIPASTO (see page 84)

BEEF, CASHEW NUT AND VEGETABLE STIR-FRY IN BLACK BEAN SAUCE (see page 114)

CHOCOLATE FUDGE SELF-SAUCING PUDDING (see page 165)

SUMMER PICNIC

FETA, OLIVE AND SUNDRIED TOMATO CALZONE (see page 100) or SUMMER CALZONE (see page 109)

ORZO PASTA SALAD (see page 72)

GINGERBREAD (see page 13)

MORNING OR AFTERNOON TEA

SCONES (see page 59) (serve with jam and whipped cream)

TINY LEMON CURD TARTLETS (see page 63)

GINGERBREAD LOAF (see page 61)

PRESERVES

APPLE AND PASSIONFRUIT JELLY

2 kg cooking apples
　(e.g. Granny Smiths)
1 cup passionfruit pulp
　(about 12 passionfruit)
2 tablespoons coarsely grated
　lemon zest
water
sugar

Peel, quarter and core apples. Cut each quarter into four pieces. Place apple, passionfruit pulp and lemon zest in a saucepan. Add sufficient water to just cover the fruit. Cover pan and bring to the boil. Reduce heat and simmer for 1 hour until apple is soft and pulpy. Strain mixture through a jelly bag. (Alternatively, to strain through muslin, place three layers of muslin over a large bowl, allowing a little slack for the weight of the fruit. Tie in place with string. Slowly tip apple from the saucepan onto the muslin cloth.) Leave to sit for 6 hours. Do not disturb this process or the jelly will turn cloudy. Measure the quantity of juice. For every cup of juice, add 1 cup of sugar. Combine juice and sugar in a saucepan. Bring to the boil. Boil vigorously for about 30 minutes or until setting point is reached. To test for setting point, drop a little jelly onto a saucer. If a skin forms as it cools, the jelly will set. On a sugar thermometer, the setting point is reached at 105°C. Use a paper towel to quickly skim any scum off the surface of the jelly. Working quickly, ladle jelly into sterilised jars. Top with cellophane jam covers and secure with a rubber band. Leave jelly to set — do not move jars until they are cold. Store in a cool, dark place. This jelly will keep for up to 1 year.

APRICOT CURD

250 g fresh ripe apricots
2 tablespoons water
¾ cup sugar
50 g butter, chopped
finely grated zest of 1 lemon
juice of 1 lemon
3 egg yolks, lightly beaten

Cut apricots in half. Remove stones. Combine apricots and water in a saucepan. Bring to the boil over a medium heat. Simmer for about 4 minutes until pulpy, stirring frequently. Tip into a sieve, then rub pulp through the sieve. Combine pulp, sugar, butter, lemon zest and juice in a double boiler or heatproof bowl. Sit it over a saucepan of simmering water. Stir until sugar has dissolved and butter has melted. Add yolks, stirring constantly until the mixture thickens. Pour into clean, sterilised jars. Seal. Cool, then refrigerate. Stored in the refrigerator, Apricot Curd will keep for up to 1 month.

APRICOT JAM

MAKES ABOUT 10 × 350 ML JARS

2.75 kg apricots, halved and stoned
10–12 apricot kernels
2½ cups water
12 cups sugar

Crack a few apricot stones and remove kernels. Put apricots, kernels and water into a preserving pan. Cook slowly until fruit is pulpy. Add sugar. Stir until dissolved. Boil briskly for 30 minutes or until setting point is reached. Pour into hot, clean, dry jars.

CHARGRILLED CAPSICUMS WITH GARLIC AND ROSEMARY

6 capsicums, any colour
¼ cup extra virgin olive oil
1 clove garlic, crushed
2 teaspoons rosemary leaves
freshly ground black pepper

Preheat oven grill. Place capsicums in a baking dish. Place about 10 cm from heat source and grill until skins blacken slightly and blister, turning occasionally. Remove from oven and cover with a baking tray until cool. Core, seed and peel capsicums. Cut into 1 cm wide strips. Place in a bowl. Combine oil, garlic and rosemary. Pour over capsicums and toss lightly to combine. Season with pepper. Covered and refrigerated, these chargrilled capsicums will keep for 3–4 days.

NOTE: Chargrilled capsicums are a delicious addition to summer salads, sandwiches, pizzas or as part of an antipasto platter (see page 84).

VARIATION
For Chargrilled Capsicums with Chilli, substitute ½ teaspoon finely chopped red chilli for the garlic and rosemary.

FETA AND OLIVE PRESERVE

MAKES 3 CUPS

2 stems rosemary about 8 cm long
¼ cup dry sundried tomatoes
300 g feta cheese
4 shallots
1 cup black olives
about 2 cups olive oil

Blanch the rosemary and sundried tomatoes in boiling water for 1 minute. Dry in a 180°C oven for 5 minutes. Cut rosemary into 4 cm lengths. Cut feta into 1 cm cubes. Peel shallots and cut into thin slices. Layer feta cheese, olives, shallot slices and sundried tomatoes into clean, dry jars. Add rosemary pieces and pour over enough olive oil to cover the cheese. Seal and store in the refrigerator for at least 2 weeks before using. Use the oil for cooking or making dressings and eat the cheese and olive mixture with crusty bread or as part of an antipasto platter (see page 84).

FIG AND ORANGE JAM

1 kg ready-soaked dried figs
finely grated zest of 2 oranges
1 cup freshly squeezed orange juice
1 litre water
2 cups sugar

Cut each fig into six pieces. Combine figs, orange zest and juice and water in a large saucepan. Bring to the boil. Simmer for 30 minutes until figs are tender. Add sugar, stirring until dissolved. Simmer for 45 minutes or until mixture is thick, stirring frequently to prevent burning. Remove from heat and allow to cool, uncovered, in the saucepan. Transfer to covered containers and refrigerate. Stored in the refrigerator, this jam will keep for up to 3 months.

NOTE: For a chunkier jam, cut figs into quarters.

HONEY AND BEER MUSTARD

½ cup white mustard seeds
2 tablespoons black mustard seeds
½ cup cider vinegar
½ cup beer
1 teaspoon salt
¼ cup liquid honey

Combine mustard seeds, vinegar and beer in a small bowl. Cover and set aside for 6–8 hours or overnight. Place in a food processor with salt and honey. Blend to desired consistency — for a smoother mustard, blend for a longer time. Pour into sterilised jars. Cover with a lid. The mustard will thicken with standing. This mustard will keep for up to 6 months.

INDIAN MANGO CHUTNEY

2 limes
3 tablespoons, approximately, salt
425 g can mango slices
2 onions
4 cloves garlic
1 tablespoon hot curry powder
2 tablespoons finely chopped root
 ginger
2 cups white vinegar
¾ cup brown sugar

Cut limes into eighths and sprinkle with salt. Leave for 1 hour. Rinse limes and dry. Drain mango slices. Peel onions and chop coarsely. Crush, peel and chop garlic. Place mango slices, limes, onions, garlic, curry powder, ginger, vinegar and brown sugar into a preserving pan. Cook mixture over a medium heat for 1 hour or until thick and pulpy. Spoon into hot, clean, dry jars. Seal when cold.

CHARGRILLED CAPSICUMS WITH GARLIC AND ROSEMARY ❧ 211

215 ❧ MARINATED OLIVES WITH HERBS

ORANGE, LIME AND GINGER MARMALADE ❧ 216

216 ❧ OVEN-DRIED TOMATOES

LEMON HONEY

MAKES ABOUT 2 × 250 ML JARS

50 g butter
¾ cup sugar
1 cup lemon juice (see page 231)
2 eggs, beaten
1 teaspoon finely grated lemon zest

Melt the butter in the top of a double boiler. Stir in sugar and lemon juice until sugar is dissolved. Add eggs and lemon zest. Place over boiling water and cook, stirring all the time until mixture thickens. Pour into hot, clean, dry jars.

MARINATED OLIVES WITH HERBS

500 g Kalamata olives
2 cloves garlic, peeled
2 bay leaves
3 sprigs of rosemary
1 teaspoon black peppercorns
300 ml pure olive oil
⅓ cup white wine vinegar

Place olives in a sieve and drain thoroughly. Cut garlic cloves in half lengthwise. Rinse bay leaves and rosemary under cold running water. Pat dry with paper towels. Pack olives into a clean, sterilised 750 ml jar, adding garlic, bay leaves, rosemary and peppercorns as you go. Combine oil and vinegar in a saucepan. Heat until warm. Pour over olives — the olives must be completely covered with the mixture. Seal jar. Store in a cool, dark place for 2–3 weeks before using. Marinated olives will keep for up to 3 months.

VARIATION
For Marinated Olives with Chilli, substitute 1 small red chilli, which has been seeded and thinly sliced, for the herbs.

MARMALADE

MAKES ABOUT 10 × 350 ML JARS

4 large grapefruit, minced, chopped
    or thinly sliced
2 lemons, minced, chopped or thinly
    sliced
3.4 litres water
sugar

Cover grapefruit and lemons with water and stand overnight. Next day, boil for 45 minutes or until fruit is soft and pulpy. Allow to cool a little. Measure pulp and return to pan. Bring to the boil. For each cup of pulp, add 1 cup sugar. Stir until dissolved. Boil briskly, stirring occasionally until setting point is reached. Pour into hot, clean, dry jars.

OLIVE TAPENADE

4 anchovy fillets
200 g pitted black olives (preferably Kalamata olives)
2 tablespoons capers, drained
2 cloves garlic, crushed
1 tablespoon lemon juice
1 teaspoon oregano leaves
½ cup extra virgin olive oil
freshly ground black pepper

Rinse anchovy fillets under cold running water. Pat dry with a paper towel. Put anchovy fillets, olives, capers, garlic, lemon juice and oregano in a food processor. Gradually add oil, pulsing until the mixture forms a coarse paste. Season with pepper. Covered and refrigerated, tapenade will keep for up to 1 week.

ORANGE, LIME AND GINGER MARMALADE

1 litre freshly squeezed orange juice
finely sliced zest of 2 oranges
juice of 6 limes
2½ cups sugar
½ cup chopped crystallised ginger

Combine orange juice, orange zest and lime juice in a large saucepan. Cover pan and bring to the boil. Simmer for 1 hour. Add sugar. Boil uncovered for 30 minutes. Remove from heat. Add ginger. Cool. Transfer to clean jars or containers. Covered and refrigerated, this marmalade will keep for up to 3 months.

OVEN-DRIED TOMATOES

acid-free or low-acid tomatoes
pure olive oil to cover

Preheat oven to 110°C. Cut tomatoes in half lengthwise. Arrange in a single layer, cut-side down, on a wire rack. Place rack over a shallow baking tray that has been lined with foil. Place tray in oven, leaving the door slightly ajar. Cook for 7–9 hours (see note below), turning the tomatoes halfway through the cooking time. Pack tomatoes in a sterilised jar. Pour in sufficient olive oil to completely cover the tomatoes. Cover jar with a lid. Refrigerated, oven-dried tomatoes will keep for up to 1 month.

NOTE: For semi-dried tomatoes, the cooking time will be about 7 hours. For fully dried tomatoes, the cooking time will be about 9 hours. These times are only estimates, as the size of the tomatoes will influence the cooking time. The oil may appear to solidify slightly when the jars of tomatoes are refrigerated. Remove from the refrigerator and allow to return to room temperature before using.

PEACH CONSERVE ◈ 218

218 ◈ PEACHES IN SPICED BRANDY

PLUM SAUCE ◈ 219

219 ◈ PRESERVED LEMONS

PEACH CONSERVE

2 cups sugar
½ cup water
¼ cup freshly squeezed lemon juice
1 kg firm, ripe peaches, peeled, stoned
   and sliced

Place sugar and water in a saucepan. Stir over a low heat until sugar has dissolved. Bring to the boil, stirring constantly. Reduce heat, add lemon juice and peaches and simmer for 5 minutes. Remove from heat and set aside for 1 hour. Reheat peaches. Bring to the boil. Reduce heat and simmer for 30 minutes until peaches are translucent and the syrup is thick. Spoon into a hot, sterilised 750 ml jar. Cover with a lid. Refrigerated, this conserve will keep for up to 3 months.

NOTE: This conserve is not as thick as jam.

PEACHES IN SPICED BRANDY

1 litre water
3 tablespoons lemon juice
12 medium firm, ripe peaches
2½ cups water
1 kg sugar
1 cinnamon stick
4 whole cloves
¾ cup brandy

Bring first measure of water and lemon juice to the boil in a saucepan. Cut peaches in half. Add peaches four at a time and cook for 1½ minutes or until liquid returns to the boil. Using a slotted spoon, transfer peaches to iced water to cool. Remove skins and stones. Combine second measure of water and the sugar in a large saucepan. Bring to the boil. Carefully add 12 peach halves to the syrup, return to the boil, reduce heat and simmer gently for 2 minutes. Using a slotted spoon, remove peaches and set aside to cool. Repeat with remaining peaches. Add cinnamon stick and cloves to the syrup. Return syrup to the boil. Boil vigorously for 20 minutes or until it reaches 105°C on a sugar thermometer. Remove cinnamon stick and cloves. Stir in brandy. Pack peaches into two clean, sterilised 1 litre jars. Pour syrup over peaches until overflowing the jar. (Peaches must be completely covered with syrup.) Seal. Stored in a cool place, these peaches will keep for up to 1 year.

PICKLED ONIONS

1.5 kg pickling onions
½ cup salt
water
3 dry chillies, approximately
6 peppercorns, approximately
malt or white vinegar

Put onions in a non-metallic bowl. Sprinkle with salt. Add cold water to cover onions. Stand for 24 hours. Drain and rinse in cold water. Drain again and pack into jars. To each jar, add 1 chilli and 2 peppercorns. Add vinegar to cover onions. Seal with non-metallic lids or corks. Store for 4–6 weeks before using.

PLUM JAM

2 kg plums, halved and stoned
1½ cups water
7 cups sugar

Put plums and water into a preserving pan. Boil until soft and pulpy. Add sugar. Stir until dissolved. Boil briskly for 15 minutes or until setting point is reached. Pour into hot, clean, dry jars.

PLUM SAUCE

2.75 kg plums
1.75 litres malt vinegar
3 cups brown sugar
8–10 cloves garlic
2 teaspoons ground pepper
2 teaspoons ground cloves
2 teaspoons ground ginger
1 teaspoon ground mace
½ teaspoon cayenne pepper
1 tablespoon salt

Put all the ingredients into a preserving pan. Bring to the boil, stirring frequently. Boil steadily until mixture is pulpy. Press through a colander or coarse sieve. Return sauce to pan and boil for 2–3 minutes. Pour into hot, clean, dry bottles and seal.

PRESERVED LEMONS

500 g small even-sized lemons
1 cup plain salt
1 cup water
½ cup sugar
1 cup cider vinegar
cinnamon sticks

Wash the lemons and halve crosswise. Place in a non-metallic bowl. Sprinkle salt over and leave for 2 days. Rinse lemons and dry. Pack into hot, clean, dry jars. Bring water, sugar, vinegar and cinnamon sticks to the boil and simmer for 5 minutes. Pour over lemons to cover. Clean rim of jar and seal. Lemons are sealed when the lid is concave.

ROASTED RED CAPSICUM AND CORIANDER PESTO

MAKES 1 CUP

2 red capsicums, roasted (see page
  232), peeled and seeded
1 cup lightly packed coriander leaves
2 cloves garlic, crushed
¼ cup toasted pine nuts (see Nuts
  page 231)
1 tablespoon extra virgin olive oil
salt and freshly ground black pepper

Roughly chop capsicums. Place in a food
processor with coriander, garlic, pine nuts and
oil. Pulse until the mixture forms a coarse
paste. Season with salt and pepper. Covered and
refrigerated, this pesto will keep for 2–3 days.

SUNDRIED TOMATO PESTO

MAKES 1½ CUPS

1 cup drained sundried tomatoes in oil
2 cloves garlic, crushed
¼ cup toasted pine nuts (see Nuts
  page 231)
¼ cup finely grated parmesan cheese
½ cup extra virgin olive oil,
  approximately
salt and freshly ground black pepper

Place sundried tomatoes, garlic, pine nuts and
parmesan in a food processor. Gradually add
oil, pulsing until the mixture forms a coarse
paste. Season with salt and pepper. Covered and
refrigerated, this pesto will keep for up to 1 week.

WALNUT PESTO

MAKES ABOUT 1½ CUPS

2 cups (225 g) quality walnut pieces
½ cup loosely packed parsley sprigs
½ cup finely grated parmesan cheese
2 cloves garlic, crushed
½ cup extra virgin olive oil
salt and freshly ground black pepper

Place walnuts, parsley, parmesan and garlic in a
food processor. Gradually add oil, pulsing until
the mixture forms a coarse paste. Season with
salt and pepper. Covered and refrigerated, this
pesto will keep for up to 1 week.

WHITE WINE AND ROSEMARY MUSTARD

MAKES 1½ CUPS

½ cup white mustard seeds
2 tablespoons black mustard seeds
½ cup white wine vinegar
½ cup dry white wine
2 tablespoons chopped rosemary
  leaves
1 teaspoon salt
¼ cup sugar

Combine mustard seeds, vinegar and wine in
a small bowl. Cover and set aside for 6–8 hours
or overnight. Place in a food processor with
rosemary, salt and sugar. Blend to desired
consistency — for a smoother mustard, blend for
a longer time. Pour into sterilised jars. Cover with
a lid. The mustard will thicken with standing.
This mustard will keep for up to 1 month.

NOTE: The addition of rosemary reduces the shelf life.

ICINGS.PASTRIES
DRESSINGS
⁊ SAUCES

BUTTER ICING

100 g butter, softened
¼ teaspoon vanilla essence
2 cups icing sugar, sifted
1–2 tablespoons hot water

Cream butter until light and fluffy. Add vanilla essence. Gradually beat in icing sugar, beating until smooth. Add sufficient water to give a spreading consistency.

BUTTERSCOTCH SAUCE

50 g butter
1 cup brown sugar
2 tablespoons golden syrup
¼ cup cream

To make the sauce, melt butter in a small saucepan. Add sugar and golden syrup and stir until sugar dissolves. Add cream and stir constantly until sauce almost comes to the boil.

CHOCOLATE ICING

Sift 1 tablespoon cocoa with the icing sugar in the White Icing recipe.

CHOCOLATE BUTTER ICING

Sift 2 tablespoons cocoa with the icing sugar in Butter Icing recipe.

COFFEE ICING

Dissolve 2 teaspoons instant coffee powder in 1 tablespoon hot water. Mix into icing sugar and proceed as for White Icing recipe.

CREAM CHEESE ICING

2 tablespoons butter, softened
¼ cup cream cheese
1 cup icing sugar
½ teaspoon grated lemon zest

Beat butter and cream cheese until creamy. Mix in icing sugar and lemon zest, beating well to combine.

LEMON ICING

In the recipe for White Icing, replace vanilla essence with 1 teaspoon grated lemon zest. Replace water with lemon juice. Add a few drops of yellow food colouring if wished.

LEMON CURD

50 g butter
¾ cup sugar
1 cup lemon juice
2 eggs, beaten
1 teaspoon finely grated lemon zest

Melt the butter in the top of a double boiler. Stir in sugar and lemon juice until sugar is dissolved. Add eggs and lemon zest. Place over boiling water and cook, stirring all the time until mixture thickens. Cool. Store in the refrigerator in a covered container.

MAKES 2 CUPS

MELTED CHOCOLATE ICING (Ganache)

200 g cooking chocolate or dark chocolate
25 g butter
½ cup cream

Break chocolate into top of a double boiler or a small heatproof bowl. Sit over simmering water. Add butter and cream. Stir constantly until melted and mixture is smooth. Set aside until cool. Beat until thick before using.

ORANGE ICING

In the recipe for White Icing, replace vanilla essence with 2 teaspoons grated orange zest. Replace water with orange juice. Add a few drops of yellow and red food colouring if wished.

WHITE ICING

2 cups icing sugar
¼ teaspoon butter, softened
2 tablespoons water, approximately
¼ teaspoon vanilla essence

Sift icing sugar into a bowl. Add butter. Add sufficient water to mix to a spreadable consistency. Flavour with vanilla essence.

FLAKY PASTRY

2 cups Edmonds high grade flour
¼ teaspoon salt
200 g butter
6 tablespoons cold water, approximately

Sift flour and salt into a bowl. Cut a quarter of the butter into the flour until it resembles fine breadcrumbs. Add sufficient water to mix to a stiff dough. On a lightly floured board, roll out dough to a rectangle 0.5–1 cm thick. With the short end of the rectangle facing you, dot two-thirds of the pastry with a third of the remaining butter to within 1 cm of the dough edge. Fold the unbuttered pastry into the middle of the pastry. Fold the buttered section over to the folded edge. Seal the edges with a rolling pin and mark the dough with the rolling pin to form corrugations. Give the pastry a quarter turn. Roll into a rectangle. Repeat twice until all the butter is used. Chill pastry for 5 minutes between rollings if possible. Use as required for savoury pies and vol au vents.

MAKES 500 G

FOOD-PROCESSOR SHORT PASTRY

Use ingredients listed for Short Pastry. Have butter and water very cold. Dice butter. Put flour in food processor. Add butter. Pulse until it resembles fine breadcrumbs. Add water by drops and pulse until mixture forms small balls. Do not overmix. Turn out onto a lightly floured surface. Knead lightly. Wrap and chill for at least 15 minutes before rolling.

NUT PASTRY

To the Sweet Shortcrust Pastry recipe, add ½ cup chopped walnuts or nuts of your choice before mixing to a stiff dough.

PUFF PASTRY

In the Flaky Pastry recipe, increase butter to 250 g. Roll and fold the pastry six times.

SHORT PASTRY

2 cups Edmonds standard grade flour
¼ teaspoon salt
125 g butter
cold water

Sift flour and salt together. Cut in the butter until it resembles fine breadcrumbs. Mix to a stiff dough with a little water. Roll out very lightly and do not handle more than is necessary. Use as required for sweet or savoury pies and tarts, and quiches.

MAKES 375 G

SPICE PASTRY

To the flour in the Sweet Shortcrust Pastry recipe, add 2 teaspoons mixed spice.

SWEET SHORTCRUST PASTRY

1 cup Edmonds standard grade flour
75 g butter
¼ cup sugar
1 egg yolk
1 tablespoon water

Sift flour. Cut in butter until it resembles fine breadcrumbs. Stir in sugar. Add egg yolk and water. Mix to a stiff dough. Chill for 30 minutes before using. Use as required for sweet pies and tarts.

MAKES ABOUT 200 G
(This pastry can be made in a food processor.)

WHOLEMEAL PASTRY

In the recipe for Short Pastry, replace flour with Edmonds wholemeal flour and add 1 teaspoon Edmonds baking powder.

AVOCADO DRESSING

1 ripe avocado, peeled and roughly chopped
juice of 1 lemon or lime
¼ cup extra virgin olive oil
½ teaspoon sugar
few drops of Tabasco sauce
salt and freshly ground black pepper

Put avocado into food processor or blender. Process until smooth. Add lime juice, oil and sugar. Process to combine. Season to taste with Tabasco, salt and pepper.

MAKES ½ CUP

BLUE CHEESE DRESSING

100 g blue vein cheese
1 cup (250 g) sour cream
  (or ¾ cup cream and ¼ cup white vinegar)
1 clove garlic, crushed
2–3 tablespoons milk

Mash cheese with fork. Add sour cream, garlic and milk. Beat or blend until smooth.

MAKES 1½ CUPS

CAESAR SALAD DRESSING

1 egg
1 anchovy, drained and roughly chopped
2 teaspoons white vinegar
1 teaspoon lemon juice
1 small clove garlic, crushed
¼ cup extra virgin olive oil
freshly ground black pepper

Cook egg in boiling water for 1 minute. Drain. Break open egg and tip into a small bowl. Add anchovy, vinegar, lemon juice and garlic. Whisk vigorously to combine. Add oil in a continuous stream, whisking constantly. Season to taste with pepper.

MAKES ⅓ CUP

FRENCH DRESSING (Vinaigrette)

¾ cup extra virgin olive oil
¼ cup white, wine or cider vinegar, or lemon juice
¼ teaspoon dry mustard
salt and freshly ground black pepper
1 clove garlic, crushed
1 tablespoon chopped parsley, chives or fresh basil

Put all ingredients into a screw-top jar. Shake well to combine.

MAKES 1 CUP

MAYONNAISE

1 egg yolk
½ teaspoon salt
¼ teaspoon dry mustard
pinch of cayenne pepper
1 tablespoon malt vinegar, or lemon juice
1 cup extra virgin olive oil

Mix egg yolk, salt, mustard and cayenne pepper in a bowl. Add vinegar. Very gradually add oil, beating constantly with a whisk or beater. As mixture begins to combine, add remaining oil in a fine stream while beating. If mixture is too thick, add more vinegar.

MAKES 1 CUP

QUICK BLENDER MAYONNAISE

2 eggs
1 tablespoon white or wine vinegar, or lemon juice
½ teaspoon dry mustard
½ teaspoon salt
pinch of cayenne pepper
1 cup extra virgin olive oil

Put eggs, vinegar, mustard, salt and cayenne pepper into food processor or blender and process until combined. Continue blending while adding oil in a thin, steady stream, blending until thick. If too thick, add extra vinegar.

MAKES 1¼ CUPS

MUSTARD DRESSING

Add 2 teaspoons wholegrain mustard to the French Dressing recipe.

UNCOOKED (Condensed Milk) SALAD DRESSING

397 g can sweetened condensed milk
1 cup malt vinegar
1 teaspoon salt
2 teaspoons dry mustard

Stir all ingredients until combined. Leave to stand for a few minutes to thicken before using.

MAKES ABOUT 2 CUPS

YOGHURT DRESSING

1 cup natural unsweetened yoghurt
1 tablespoon lemon juice
¼ teaspoon dry mustard
salt and freshly ground black pepper

Stir all ingredients until combined.
Chill before using.

MAKES 1 CUP

APPLE SAUCE

3–4 large cooking apples, peeled and chopped
1 tablespoon water
1 tablespoon butter
2 cloves or few drops lemon juice
sugar to taste

Put apples, water, butter and cloves into a
saucepan. Simmer until apples are pulped.
Blend or beat with a fork until smooth. Add
sugar to taste.

MAKES ABOUT 1½ CUPS

BÉARNAISE SAUCE

3 tablespoons wine vinegar or tarragon vinegar
6 peppercorns
1 bay leaf
¼ small onion, chopped
2 egg yolks
75–100 g butter
salt and freshly ground black pepper
1 tablespoon chopped parsley

Put vinegar, peppercorns, bay leaf and
onion into a small saucepan. Bring to the
boil and reduce to 1 tablespoon. Strain and
reserve liquid. Place yolks and reserved
liquid in a double boiler and lightly beat.
Gradually add butter in small pieces,
beating until sauce is thick enough to show
the marks of whisk. Do not allow to boil or
sauce will curdle. Season to taste with salt
and pepper. Add parsley. Keep warm.

MAKES ABOUT ¾ CUP

BÉCHAMEL SAUCE

Stud an onion with 6 cloves. Place onion
in 1 cup milk and bring almost to the
boil. Strain. In a separate pan, melt
2 tablespoons butter and continue as
for White Sauce recipe. Add heated milk.

CHEESE SAUCE

After cooking White Sauce, remove pan
from heat. Stir in ½ cup grated tasty
cheddar cheese.

CUCUMBER AND MINT RAITA

¾ cup natural unsweetened yoghurt
½ cup grated telegraph cucumber
1 tablespoon chopped mint
salt and freshly ground black pepper

Combine all ingredients in a bowl. Mix well.

MAKES ABOUT 1¼ CUPS

CURRY SAUCE

In the White Sauce recipe, include
1–2 teaspoons curry powder when adding
flour.

GREEN PEPPERCORN SAUCE

50 g butter
2 tablespoons lemon juice
2 tablespoons green peppercorns, rinsed
4 egg yolks
¼ cup cream
1 teaspoon prepared mustard
salt and freshly ground black pepper

Melt butter in a saucepan. Add lemon juice.
Stir in peppercorns, egg yolks, cream and
mustard. Cook over gentle heat until sauce
thickens. Do not allow sauce to boil. Season
to taste with salt and pepper.

MAKES ¾ CUP

HOLLANDAISE SAUCE

50 g butter
1 tablespoon lemon juice
2 egg yolks
¼ cup cream
½ teaspoon dry mustard
¼ teaspoon salt

Melt the butter in a double boiler. Add
lemon juice, egg yolks and cream. Cook,
stirring constantly, until thick and smooth.
Do not boil or sauce will curdle. Remove
from heat. Add mustard and salt and beat
until smooth.

MAKES ¾ CUP

ONION SAUCE

Add 1 sliced onion to butter in the White Sauce recipe and cook until soft. Continue method.

PARSLEY SAUCE

After cooking White Sauce, remove pan from heat. Add 2–4 tablespoons chopped parsley.

PESTO

1 tablespoon extra virgin olive oil
2 tablespoons pine nuts
3 cloves garlic, chopped
2 cups fresh basil leaves
¼ cup extra virgin olive oil
salt and pepper

Heat first measure of oil in a small frying pan. Add pine nuts and cook, stirring frequently, until golden. Drain on absorbent paper. Put the garlic, basil and pine nuts into the bowl of a food processor or blender. Process until finely chopped. Continue processing while adding second measure of oil in a thin, steady stream. Process for a few seconds until just combined. Season with salt and pepper to taste.

MAKES ABOUT ½ CUP

Pesto is superb tossed through hot pasta or used as a tasty spread. The sauce can be frozen, but the texture will alter slightly.

SATAY SAUCE

2 tablespoons canola oil
1 clove garlic, crushed
1 onion, chopped
¼–½ teaspoon chilli powder
   (according to taste)
½ cup crunchy peanut butter
1 tablespoon soy sauce
1 tablespoon brown sugar
¾ cup coconut cream
salt and freshly ground black pepper

Heat oil in a saucepan. Add garlic, onion and chilli powder. Cook until onion is clear. Stir in peanut butter, soy sauce and sugar. Add coconut cream. Cook until mixture boils, stirring constantly. Season to taste with salt and pepper.

MAKES 1¼ CUPS

SPICY BARBECUE SAUCE

1 cup tomato sauce
½ cup water
3 tablespoons golden syrup
1 teaspoon salt
2 teaspoons Worcestershire sauce
½ teaspoon curry powder
freshly ground black pepper
1 clove garlic, crushed
¼ cup dry red wine

Combine all ingredients. Leave to stand for 5–6 hours.

MAKES 2 CUPS

TARTARE SAUCE

1 cup Mayonnaise (see page 225)
1 tablespoon chopped parsley
1 tablespoon finely chopped capers or
   gherkins
1 tablespoon finely chopped onion

Combine all ingredients.

MAKES 1 CUP

WHITE SAUCE

2 tablespoons butter
2 tablespoons Edmonds standard grade flour
1 cup milk
salt and freshly ground black pepper

Melt butter in a small saucepan. Add flour and stir constantly for 2 minutes. Remove from heat. Gradually add milk, stirring constantly. Return pan to the heat, stirring continuously until sauce thickens and comes to the boil. Season to taste with salt and pepper.

MAKES 1 CUP

WEIGHTS AND MEASURES

New Zealand Standard metric cup and spoon measures are used in all recipes.

ALL MEASUREMENTS ARE LEVEL

Easy measuring — use measuring cups or jugs for liquid measures and sets of 1 cup, ½ cup, ⅓ cup and ¼ cup for dry ingredients.

Brown sugar measurements — are firmly packed so that the sugar will hold the shape of the cup when tipped out.

Eggs — no. 6 eggs are used as the standard size.

ABBREVIATIONS

l	=	litre
ml	=	millilitre
cm	=	centimetre
mm	=	millimetre
g	–	gram
kg	=	kilogram
°C	=	degrees Celsius

STANDARD MEASURES

1 cup	=	250 millilitres
1 litre	=	4 cups
1 tablespoon	=	15 millilitres
1 dessertspoon	=	10 millilitres
1 teaspoon	=	5 millilitres
½ teaspoon	=	2.5 millilitres
¼ teaspoon	=	1.25 millilitres

APPROXIMATE METRIC/IMPERIAL CONVERSIONS WEIGHT

25 g	=	1 ounce
125 g	=	4 ounces
225 g	=	8 ounces
500 g	=	1 pound
1 kg	=	2¼ pounds

VOLUME

1 litre	=	1¾ pints

MEASUREMENTS

1 cm	=	½ inch
20 cm	=	8 inches
30 cm	=	12 inches

IN COMMON COOKING USE

WEIGHTS AND MEASURES — APPROXIMATE EQUIVALENTS

ITEM	MEASURE	WEIGHT
breadcrumbs (fresh)	1 cup	50 g
butter	2 tablespoons	30 g
cheese (grated, firmly packed)	1 cup	100 g
cocoa	4 tablespoons	25 g
coconut	1 cup	75 g
cornflour	4 tablespoons	25 g
cream	½ pint	300 ml
dried fruit (currants, sultanas, raisins, dates)	1 cup	150–175 g
flour	1 cup	125 g
golden syrup	1 tablespoon	25 g
milk	1 cup	250 ml
oil	1 tablespoon	15 ml
rice, sago	2 tablespoons	25 g
	1 cup	200 g
salt	2 tablespoons	25 g
sugar, white	2 tablespoons	30 g
	1 cup	250 g
sugar, brown	1 cup (firmly packed)	200 g
	1 cup (loosely packed)	125–150 g
sugar, icing	1 cup	150 g
standard no. 6 egg		about 50 g

BEFORE AND AFTER EQUIVALENT MEASURES

APPROXIMATE AMOUNTS NEEDED TO GIVE MEASURES:

⅓ cup uncooked rice   = 1 cup cooked rice
⅓ cup uncooked pasta   = 1 cup cooked pasta
2–3 chicken pieces   = 1 cup cooked chicken
100 g cheese   = 1 cup grated cheese
75 g mushrooms   = 1 cup sliced mushrooms = ½ cup cooked mushrooms
4 toast slices bread   = 1 cup fresh beadcrumbs
200 g (two) potatoes   = 1 cup mashed potato

OVEN CONVERSIONS

160°C = 325°F
180°C = 350°F
190°C = 375°F
200°C = 400°F

A GUIDE TO OVEN TEMPERATURES AND USE

PRODUCT	°C	°F	GAS NO.	DESCRIPTION
meringues, pavlova	110–140	225–275	¼–1	slow
custards, milk puddings, shortbread, rich fruit cakes, casseroles, slow roasting	150–160	300–325	2–3	moderately slow
biscuits, large and small cakes	180–190	350–375	4–5	moderate
roasting, sponges, muffins, short pastry	190–220	375–425	5–6	moderately hot
flaky pastry, scones, browning toppings	220–230	425–450	6–8	hot
puff pastry	250–260	475–500	9–10	very hot

OVEN HINTS

Oven racks — position before turning oven on.

OVEN POSITIONS

Bottom of oven	use for slow cooking and low temperature cooking
Middle of oven	for moderate temperature cooking
Above middle	for quick cooking and high temperature cooking
Fan-forced ovens	refer to the manufacturer's directions as the models vary.

Preheat oven to required temperature before food preparation.
Cooking temperatures and times are a guide only as ovens may vary.

GLOSSARY

Al dente: Used to describe cooked pasta that is firm to the bite.

Arborio rice is a short-grain rice predominantly grown in Italy. It is used as the basis of Italian-style risotto dishes. As Arborio rice cooks, the starch released from the granule thickens the sauce, giving a creamy consistency.

Bain-marie is a water bath. The dish of food to be cooked is placed in a larger dish and surrounded with hot water to come half to three-quarters of the way up the food dish. This provides a gentle, more even heat for mixtures that are sensitive to direct heat.

Bake blind: To place a piece of baking paper in an unbaked pastry case, fill with dried beans or rice and bake. This enables the pastry to bake with a flat base. Beans or rice for baking blind can be stored and re-used.

Baking paper has a special coating on it to prevent sticking. It saves greasing tins or baking trays. For cake or slice tins, line the base of the tin with baking paper. There is no need to grease the sides of the tin. Once the food is cooked, run a knife around the edges of the tin, pressing the knife blade against the tin to prevent damaging the cake or slice. Cover baking trays with baking paper to save greasing when baking biscuits.

Baking powder is a mixture of cream of tartar and baking soda plus wheat fillers, which helps the baking powder to flow easily.

Baking soda is also known as bicarbonate of soda.

Balsamic vinegar, a specialty of Modena, Italy, is thick, dark vintage vinegar with a sweet-and-sour flavour, which is traditionally matured in oak. It is used in salad dressings, marinades and sauces.

Basmati rice is an aromatic long-grain rice with a nutty flavour. Basmati rice is used extensively in Indian cuisine.

Baste: To spoon juices or marinades over foods being roasted to prevent drying and to give a glossy surface.

Blanch: To place fruit and vegetables in boiling water briefly, then remove to cold water to ease removing of skins or prepare for freezing.

Blend: To mix ingredients thoroughly to get an even consistency.

Boil: To cook at boiling point with large rolling bubbles forming.

Bouquet garni is a mixture of parsley, thyme and bay leaf, which is tied together with cotton if fresh herbs are used, or enclosed in a muslin bag if dried herbs are used. Bouquet garni is used as a flavouring for stocks. It should be removed once the cooking is completed.

Braise: To gently fry in fat, then cook slowly in very little moisture, covered.

Chicken: To test whether chicken is cooked, pierce it in the thickest part with a skewer, satay stick or sharp knife. If the juices run clear, the chicken is cooked. If the juices are pink, further cooking is necessary.

Chilli oil is oil flavoured with fresh chillies. It can be bought already flavoured or fresh chillies can be steeped in oil to flavour your own. Use any oil you prefer, depending on its end use.

Chocolate curls are easily made using a potato peeler and 'peeling' a piece of chocolate. Well-formed curls will be made if the chocolate is slightly soft.

Clarified butter is butter from which milk solids have been removed. Can be used for frying as it heats to a high temperature without burning. Known also as frying butter or ghee.

Coconut throughout this cookbook means desiccated unless otherwise stated. Coconut can be toasted by heating it in a frying pan over a moderate heat. Shake the pan from time to time. Remove pan from heat when coconut just starts to colour.

Coconut cream or coconut milk is available canned or powdered, or can be made by mixing 1¼ cups of coconut with 300 ml of boiling water, then straining through a sieve and reserving the liquid. This will give about 1 cup (250 ml) of coconut milk.

Cold-smoked salmon has a translucent look and is smoked without heat.

Cool pastry fillings: Cold fillings should be used in pastry shells to prevent pastry becoming soggy on the bottom.

Cornflour is made from maize and is a starch used to thicken products such as sauces and desserts, or it can be used in some baked products.

Couscous is fluffy grains of semolina, which are steamed and served like rice. Couscous is used extensively in Moroccan cooking.

Cream: To beat softened butter or other fat with sugar until light, fluffy and creamy in colour.

Curry powder is a mixture of spices and you can combine different spices in different amounts to make your own blend. Some of the basic spices might include cumin, coriander, ginger, cloves, fenugreek, turmeric and cinnamon. Whole spices can be ground with a mortar and pestle, or prepared ground spices can be used.

Cut in: Using a knife, pastry blender, food processor or clean fingertips to combine fat with flour to get a crumb-like consistency.

Eggs should be at room temperature when making sponges and other baked goods as this produces a cake with better volume. Egg whites for making meringues and pavlovas should always be at room temperature.

Filo pastry is tissue-paper-thin pastry traditionally used for strudels. It can be bought in packets from the supermarket and once opened should be used within a week to 10 days. When working with filo pastry (sometimes written as phyllo) place it under a damp teatowel to prevent it from drying out and becoming brittle and hard to manage.

Flour: As a rule of thumb, use standard grade flour for baking and high grade flour for pastry, breads, doughs and heavy fruit cakes.

Fold: Combining a delicate mixture with a heavier one by using a metal spoon in a cutting action, cutting down through centre and bringing bottom mixture to top. Used for additions of whipped cream and beaten egg whites.

Fresh and dried herbs: As a rule of thumb, replace a measure of fresh herbs with half the quantity of dried herbs. Double a dried measure if replacing with fresh herbs.

Fresh ginger is root ginger. This is available from the fruit and vegetables section of the supermarket and should be stored in the refrigerator crisper or frozen for easy grating. The ginger root can be peeled before using if wished.

Frothy: When making white sauce, heat butter and flour until mixture appears frothy with small bubbles before adding liquid.

Hokkien noodles are wheat-based Chinese noodles used in Asian cuisine. They are ideal for use in stir-fries, soups and salads and can be purchased from the Asian or noodle section of most supermarkets.

Hot-smoked salmon has the look of cooked fish and has been smoked with heat.

Jelly bag: A muslin or fine cloth bag that can be hung to allow jelly to drain through when preserving. A piece of muslin can be used for the same task. Attach this to the legs of an upturned chair before the jelly is drained through.

Julienne: To cut ingredients, usually root vegetables and citrus rinds, into very thin sticks; often used as a garnish.

Knead: To press non-yeast doughs together to get an even texture. Yeast doughs are stretched and folded to develop elasticity. This is done by pushing the dough away from you with the heel of your hand, then folding the dough over.

Lemons: Two main lemon types are grown in New Zealand — Meyer and Lisbon. Meyer lemons have a soft bright yellow flesh and semi-sweet flavour. They make a good garnish but do not have a lot of flavour in cooking. Lisbon lemons have a light, hard skin, a light lemon flesh and a sharper lemon taste. They should always be used in cooking where setting is required, as in condensed-milk cheesecakes, lemon honey and lemon meringue pies.

Mascarpone is Italian in origin and is used extensively for desserts. It can be found in the refrigerated section of most supermarkets.

Margarine can replace butter, giving a similar result. Extra flour may need to be added in some baked recipes to give the required consistency.

Marinate: To leave meat, poultry or fish in a tenderising or flavouring liquid (the marinade) for a period of time.

Mash: Food is crushed until soft. This can be done with a fork or a potato masher.

Measuring: All recipes in this book have been developed using standard metric measuring cups and spoons. All measurements are level. For easiest measuring, use measuring cups or jugs for liquid measures and sets of 1 cup, ½ cup and ¼ cup for dry ingredients. Brown sugar measures are firmly packed so that the sugar will hold the shape of the cup when tipped out.

Naan, an Indian bread, is available from Indian restaurants or from some supermarket freezers. Naan bread mixes are also available.

Nori is a type of edible seaweed sold in thin strips or sheets. It is mainly used for sushi rolls, but can also be crumbled and used to season soups, noodles or rice. It is available in the Asian food section of most supermarkets, or from Asian food stores.

Nuts can be toasted in the oven or in a pan on top of the stove. To toast nuts in the oven, place in an oven dish and cook at 180°C for 5–15 minutes, depending on the nuts. To toast on top of the stove, place nuts in a frying pan and cook over a moderate heat until just starting to colour. Toss nuts during cooking to prevent burning.

Olive oil is available in a variety of types. Light olive oil has the least flavour, with the deeper green virgin olive oils having a distinct flavour. Use olive oil to make French dressing or vinaigrette. If using olive oil in cooking, take care not to overheat it as it will smoke at a lower temperature than many oils.

Polenta is a ground corn (cornmeal), which is a staple food of northern Italy. It is boiled in water, producing a thick porridge-like mixture, which is then left to solidify.

Prepared mustard is wet mustard that has already been made or bought. Wholeseed (wholegrain) or smooth varieties are available.

Purée: Cooked fruit or vegetables mashed or sieved to give a smooth semi-liquid product.

Roasted capsicums: Cut capsicums in half lengthwise. Remove core and place cut-side down on a baking tray. Bake at 200°C for 15 minutes or until skins are blistered and browned. When capsicums are cool enough to handle, remove skin. The skins on red and yellow capsicums will blister and come away more easily than green capsicums.

Rub in: To mix fat into flour by rubbing with fingers to get a crumb-like mixture.

Sambal oelek is a paste made from hot chillies and salt.

Sauté: To fry food in a small amount of hot fat quickly and with shaking or stirring of pan to get even cooking.

Scald: Liquids are brought to boiling point.

Shallots are small brown-skinned onions similar in shape to a chestnut or large, slightly flat garlic clove. They have a mild onion flavour and are good for use in salads, dressings and casseroles or anything that requires a milder onion flavour.

Shanghai choy is a green leafy Asian vegetable. It is similar to bok choy, but has a smaller leaf. It can be found in the fruit and vegetable section of selected supermarkets or from fruit and vegetable suppliers.

Shards are long pointed pieces that look like broken glass. Praline is often broken into shards for impressive decoration.

Sieve: To pass through a mesh to get an even consistency.

Sift: To pass dry ingredients through a mesh to remove lumps and/or foreign matter, or to mix evenly.

Simmer: To cook just at boiling point, not a full rolling boil.

Skim: To remove fat or scum from the surface of a liquid with a slotted spoon, spoon or absorbent paper.

Soft breadcrumbs are made from stale bread. They are not toasted.

Softened butter makes creaming butter and sugar easy. Butter can be softened in the microwave, left to stand in a warm place or softened over hot water. Softened butter is not the same as melted butter.

Spoons: A wooden spoon is used for stirring a heated mixture, as it does not become too hot to handle. It does not discolour pale mixtures as a metal one can do by scraping against the metal of the saucepan. Metal spoons, solid or slotted, are used for transferring foods; slotted ones will allow liquids to drain from solids. Slotted spoons are useful for folding mixtures together. A metal spoon is best for folding or creaming butter and sugar by hand.

Stiffly beaten egg white: Beaten until peaks formed will hold their shape, but tips bend over. Mixture should be glossy.

Stir-fry: To stir and toss prepared ingredients in hot oil very quickly, resulting in moist meats and crisp vegetables.

Stock can be home-made or bought in cartons as a liquid, in pots as a powder or as foil-wrapped cubes. One stock cube is the equivalent of 1 teaspoon of stock powder.

Tahini is a paste made from toasted sesame seeds and is widely used in Middle Eastern cooking. It has a toasted-nut flavour.

Tepid: This is blood temperature, i.e. 37°C, and liquid feels neither hot nor cold when a drop is placed on the back of your hand.

Thick and glossy: When making meringue, egg whites and sugar are beaten until very stiff. This is when peaks stand up after the beaters are removed. The meringue should look shiny. An electric mixer should be used for this as it takes time and is too arduous to do by hand successfully. The sugar should be dissolved in the egg whites. Test by rubbing a little mixture between your fingers.

To cover steamed puddings: Tear a sheet of foil about 5 cm larger than the top of the basin. Make a pleat right across the sheet of foil. Cover basin with foil. Tie string very tightly around pudding basin just under the lip. Take a separate piece of string about 40 cm in length and fold in half. Secure the string at opposite ends of the basin to make a handle. This helps get the pudding basin in and out of the saucepan.

Tomato paste is concentrated tomato purée.

Tomato purée is available in cans or can be made from fresh tomatoes in a blender or food processor.

Wasabi is made from the thick green root of an aquatic plant grown in Japan. A basic ingredient in sushi, it is usually sold as a paste, or powder to mix with water, and can also be mixed with soy sauce and used as a dip.

Yeast is used to raise bread, etc — 1 tablespoon of Edmonds active yeast (dried granules) equals 2 tablespoons of Edmonds Surebake active yeast mixture.

Zest is the coloured outer rind of citrus fruits. It can be finely sliced (julienned) or grated and used for flavouring or as a garnish.

INDEX